LEARNING ADVENTURES IN READING

Grades 3–4

By the Staff of Score@Kaplan

Foreword by Alan Tripp

Simon & Schuster

This series is dedicated to our Score@Kaplan parents and children—thank you for making these books possible.

Published by
Kaplan Educational Centers and Simon & Schuster
1230 Avenue of the Americas
New York, NY 10020

Special thanks to: Elissa Grayer, Doreen Beauregard, Julie Schmidt, Rebecca Geller Schwartz, Linda Lott, Janet Cassidy, Marlene Greil, Nancy McDonald, Sarah Jane Bryan, Chris Wilsdon, Janet Montal, Jeannette Sanderson, David Stienecker, Dan Greenberg, Kathy Wilmore, Dorrie Berkowitz, Brent Gallenberger and Molly Walsh

Head Coach and General Manager, Score@Kaplan: Alan Tripp
President, Score@Kaplan: Robert L. Waldron
Series Content and Development: Mega-Books
Project Editor: Mary Pearce
Production Editor: Donna Mackay, Graphic Circle Inc.
Art Director: Elana Goren-Totino
Illustrators: Rick Brown, Ryan Brown, Sandy Forrest, Larry Nolte,
Evan Polenghi, Fred Schrier, Peter Spacek, Arnie Ten
Cover Design: Cheung Tai
Cover Photograph: Michael Britto

Manufactured in the United States of America
Published Simultaneously in Canada

January 1998
10 9 8 7 6 5 4 3 2 1

ISBN:0-684-84434-6

Contents

Dear Parents,

Your child's success in school is important to you, and at Score@Kaplan we are always pleased when the kids who attend our educational centers do well on their report cards. But what we really want for our kids is not just good grades. We also want everything that good grades are supposed to represent:

- We want our kids to master the key communication systems that make civilization possible: language (spoken and written), math, the visual arts, and music.
- We want them to build their critical-thinking skills so they can understand, appreciate, and improve their world.
- We want them to continually increase their knowledge and to value learning as the key to a happy, successful life.
- We want them to always do their best, to persist when challenged, to be a force for good, and to help others whenever they can.

These are ambitious goals, but our children deserve no less. We at Score@Kaplan have already helped thousands of children across the country in our centers, and we hope this series of books for children in first through sixth grades will reach many more households.

Simple Principles

We owe the remarkable success of Score@Kaplan to a few simple principles. This book was developed with these principles in mind.

- We expect every child to succeed.
- We make it possible for every child to succeed.
- We reinforce every instance of success, no matter how small.

Assessing Your Child

One helpful approach in assessing your child's skills is to ask yourself the following questions.

- How much is my child reading? At what level of difficulty?
- Has my child mastered appropriate language arts skills, such as spelling, grammar, and syntax?
- Does my child have the ability to express appropriately complex thoughts when speaking or writing?
- Does my child demonstrate mastery of all age-appropriate math skills, such as mastery of addition and subtraction facts, multiplication tables, division rules, and so on?

These questions are a good starting place and may give you new insights into your child's academic situation.

What's Going on at School

Parents will always need to monitor the situation at school and take responsibility for their child's learning. You should find out what your child should be learning at each grade level and match that against what your child actually learns.

The activity pages in *Learning Adventures* were developed using the standards developed by the professional teachers associations. As your child explores the activities in *Learning Adventures*, you might find that a particular concept hasn't been taught in school or hasn't yet been mastered by your child. This presents a great opportunity for both of you. Together you can learn something new.

Encouraging Your Child to Learn at Home

This book is full of fun learning activities you can do with your child to build understanding of key concepts in language arts, math, and science. Most activities are designed for your child to do independently. But that doesn't mean that you can't work on them together or invite your child to share the work with you. As you help your child learn, please bear in mind the following observations drawn from experience in our centers:

- Positive reinforcement is the key. Try to maintain a ratio of at least five positive remarks to every negative one.
- All praise must be genuine. Try praises such as: "That was a good try," "You got this part of it right," or "I'm proud of you for doing your best, even though it was hard."
- When a child gets stuck, giving the answer is often not the most efficient way to help. Ask open-ended questions, or rephrase the problem.
- Remember to be patient and supportive. Children need to learn that hard work pays off.

There's More to Life Than Academic Learning

Most parents recognize that academic excellence is just one of the many things they would like to ensure for their children. At Score@Kaplan, we are committed to developing the whole child. These books are designed to emphasize academic skills and critical thinking, as well as provide an opportunity for positive reinforcement and encouragement from you, the parent.

We wish you a successful and rewarding experience as you and your child embark upon this learning adventure together.

Alan Tripp
General Manager
Score@Kaplan

Dear Kids,

Get your pencils sharpened and put your game face on! You're about to start a Learning Adventure. This book is filled with puzzles, games, riddles, and lots of other fun stuff. You can do them alone or with your family and friends. While you're at it, you'll exercise your brain.

If you get stuck on something, look for the Score coaches. Think of them as your personal brain trainers. You can also check your answers on pages 65–70, if you really have to.

We know you will do a great job. That's why we have a special puzzle inside. After you do three or four pages, you'll see a puzzle piece. Cut it out, then glue it or tape it in place on page 64. When you're done with the book, the puzzle will be done, too. Then you'll find a secret message from us.

So, pump up your mind muscles and get ready to Score. You'll have a blast and boost your brain power at the same time.

Go for it!

Your Coaches at Score

Phonics and Spelling

Recognize vowel sounds and vowel combinations

NAME ______________________________

Silly Sentences

Billy loves to write silly sentences. Help him write some by choosing a word from each column and then putting the words together to make a silly sentence. There's only one trick—all of the words in a sentence must have the same vowel sound! Then, draw a picture in the box to show what the sentence means.

Crazy	fish	hide	big	maids.
Sad	beans	tap	sweet	rap.
Six	snakes	kiss	bad	times.
Shy	crabs	meet	five	peas.
Green	flies	chase	brave	lips.

1. ______________________________
2. ______________________________
3. ______________________________
4. ______________________________
5. ______________________________

1.	2.	3.

4.	5.

You may want to circle all the words with the same vowel sound with a particular color crayon.

Phonics and Spelling

Identify beginning and ending consonant blends

NAME ______________________________

Blending the Blizzard

Blaine is craving a blueberry blizzard. He has all the ingredients ready, but he needs a blender to mix them. Help Blaine make his delicious dessert by coloring the boxes that show the path to the blender. Begin at Start, and read the word in each box. If the word begins with a consonant blend, color in the box. When you're finished, you'll have a path to the blender.

A *consonant* blend is two or more consonants that blend together to make a sound. In these words, the underlined letters are consonant blends: <u>br</u>ight, <u>cr</u>anberry, <u>bl</u>ister, <u>tr</u>icycle, <u>pl</u>anet.

START

snow	bricks	candy	sunshine	jewel
right	twins	trail	nap	case
puppy	lips	class	slide	crash
tent	table	beast	dip	plant
print	bread	trick	straw	clown
star	list	nose	button	mouse
glass	flag	prize	laugh	pet

FINISH

Check Yourself: Did you make it to the blender in exactly 17 words? If not, you've taken the wrong path and need to look at the beginning of each word again.

NAME ______________________________

Syllable Search

Felipe received a letter from his friend Sonya but he's having trouble reading it. That's because Sonya made a puzzle out of her note. The number next to each blank tells you how many syllables the word for that blank has. Choose a word from the box that makes sense in the sentence and has the right number of syllables. Write it in the blank.

One way to figure out how many syllables a word has is to put your hand on your chin as you read each word. Every time your chin moves, you've said a syllable.

You're a syllable superstar! Now take a look at the puzzle piece. Glue or tape it in the correct place in the frame on page 64.

Dear Felipe,

Well, we finally made it to Camp Redwing. We drove to our (2) ____________ late last night. The first thing we did was set up the (1) __________ . Then we roasted (3) ______________ .

The (2) ____________ are simply amazing. Today we climbed all the way to the highest peak. We stopped for a (2) __________ lunch halfway up. Then we went for a quick swim in a nearby (2) ____________ . Belinda dropped her stuffed (1) __________ into the water, but it was no big deal. Before the day was over, she had seen so many real animals that she forgot all about it. As the sun began to set, we noticed a (4) ______________ flying by. The (2) ____________ even waved to us.

Tomorrow, we're going bird-watching. Good thing I brought my (4) ______________________ .

See you when I get back.

Sonya

jet	picnic	camera	marshmallows
tents	pilot	animals	mountains
bear	guide	campsite	helicopter
lake	river	hot dogs	binoculars

NAME ____

A Pair of Pears

Each pear on the left would like to be paired up with a pear on the right. Can you find the pears that belong together? You'll know they make a good pair because the words inside will be homophones. Draw lines to show the pears that go together.

Homophones are words that sound alike, but have different spellings and different meanings. Some examples are *write* and *right* and *sun* and *son*.

NAME ____

Rollerblading Races

Are you ready for a rollerblade race? Play this game with a friend and see who can make it to the rollerblading rink first. All you'll need is a penny to toss and a button or small object for each player.

How to Play:

1. Take turns tossing the penny. If it lands heads up, move 1 space. If it lands tails up, move 2 spaces.
2. When you land in a blank space, just wait for your next turn.
3. When you land in a space with 2 words, study the words carefully. If they are synonyms, move 2 spaces forward. If they are antonyms, move 2 spaces back.
4. The first player to reach the rollerblading rink wins.

Words that have the same or nearly the same meaning are called *synonyms*. Words that have opposite meanings are called *antonyms*.

Great Job! Now cut out your puzzle piece and put it in place on page 64.

START

big large

happy sad

yell shout

slow fast

loud noisy

nice kind

little small

over under

wet dry

beautiful pretty

Rhonda's Roller-blade Rink

Vocabulary

Identify compound words

NAME ____

Compound Search

Look at the pictures below. The name of each one is a compound word. Find and circle each one in the puzzle. Words can go across or down, and one word is even written backwards.

A *compound word* is a word made up of two smaller words, such as *bedtime, sunshine,* and *headache.*

You can figure out the meaning of a compound word by thinking about what each part means.

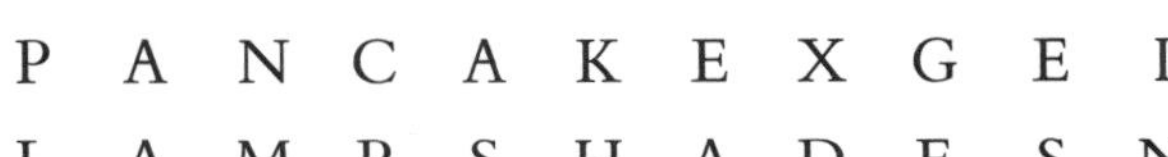

B	A	C	K	P	A	C	K	L	S	F
O	A	C	F	S	G	H	L	M	U	I
O	B	B	A	T	H	T	U	B	N	N
K	U	D	U	T	R	I	N	N	G	G
M	A	I	L	M	A	N	C	O	L	E
A	W	E	C	A	Z	J	H	P	A	R
R	A	I	N	B	O	W	B	Q	S	P
K	X	E	D	B	Y	K	O	F	S	R
P	A	N	C	A	K	E	X	G	E	I
L	A	M	P	S	H	A	D	E	S	N
B	R	D	S	P	Q	E	A	D	A	T
L	T	S	A	F	K	A	E	R	B	H

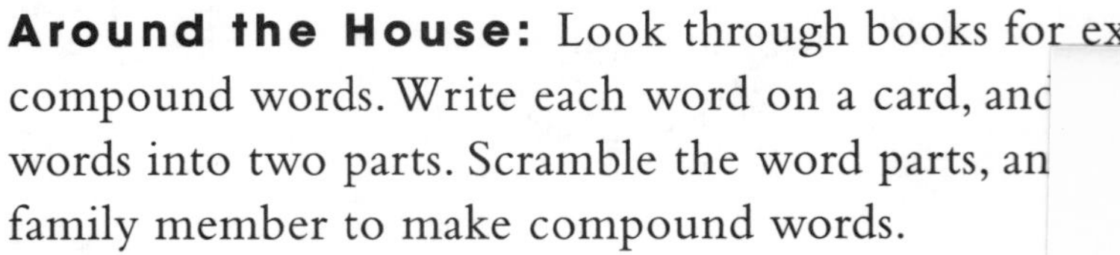

Around the House: Look through books for examples of compound words. Write each word on a card, and words into two parts. Scramble the word parts, an family member to make compound words.

NAME________________________________

Predictions by Priscilla

Priscilla is a predictor. Can you help her make predictions about these situations? What do you think will happen? Write your predictions on another piece of paper. We've made one prediction for you.

1. Juan is reading a story to the class. Ben shoots a paper airplane that bounces off Juan's face and is heading straight for the teacher. The paper airplane hits the teacher and Ben ends up in big trouble.

2. Ming Li is blowing a bubble with her Super Smackers Bubble Gum. She's trying to break the record for biggest bubble ever blown.

3. Brooke is running backwards to catch a ball. She doesn't see the ditch behind her.

4. Jeff and Carrie are making a cake. They accidentally use five cups of salt instead of sugar.

5. Todd, Ryan, and Zach are having a milk chug-a-lugging contest. Todd is drinking his milk and tipping his chair.

6. Mary Alice is running down the block to Rebecca's house. She doesn't see a banana peel and a big puddle of water on the sidewalk.

When you make a *prediction*, you use information such as words, pictures, and things you have learned in the past, to try and figure out what might happen next.

Priscilla predicts that you're a real prediction pro! Now cut out the puzzle piece. Tape or glue it in the puzzle frame on page 64.

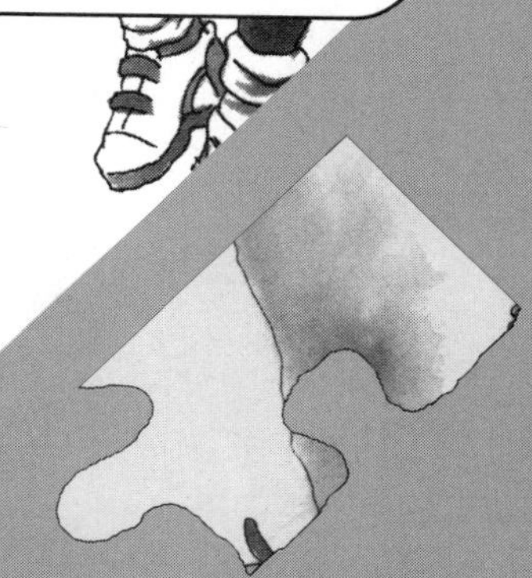

Around the House: It's fun to make predictions. Try it when you read a book. Before you get to the end of the story, try to predict what the ending will be. See how often you are right.

NAME ____________________

What's It About?

Cassie had a wacky field trip to the zoo today. She wants to tell her mom about it, but Mom's late for an appointment and has only a minute to listen. Read Cassie's description of the unusual event. On another sheet of paper, write a summary that she can share with her mom before she has to go.

A *summary* is a brief explanation. It gives all the important parts of a story but does not include small details.

The Animal Parade

I've been to the zoo a million times, but I've never seen anything like what I saw today. As we stood outside the gorilla's cage, the zookeeper went inside to put out fresh food and water. When the zookeeper bent down, that gorilla took the keys right out of his pocket! As soon as the zookeeper left, the gorilla let himself out of his cage. My class and I followed along quietly to see what would happen next.

The zookeeper went to clean the elephant's cage. While he wasn't looking, the gorilla let the elephant out of the cage. So there we were—the gorilla following the zookeeper, the elephant following the gorilla, and a classful of fourth graders following the elephant. Next, we walked by the lion's den, and what do you think happened? You-know-who let the lion loose, and the lion joined in the parade. One by one, the gorilla freed the rhinoceros, the toucan, and the polar bear. We were quite a sight walking through the zoo as an animal parade.

Finally, it was time to leave, so we turned around and headed for our bus. And can you guess who followed us? Our teacher wasn't very happy. He took the keys from the gorilla and marched every single one of those animals right back to their cages.

NAME ____

Travel Troubles

The Hernandez family had quite a vacation this year. Read Martina's diary to find out about some of the things that happened. Then underline the cause and circle the effect in each diary entry. One has been started for you.

Day 1

Dear Diary,
We didn't get to World o' Wax Balls today because my little brother let his favorite stuffed animal fly out of the car window. We had to make a pit stop at Stuff 'n Bears to get him a new one.

Day 2

Dear Diary,
This morning we had breakfast at Pancake Planet. I ate 25 chocolate chip pancakes with syrup. Now, I don't feel so good. I'll never eat another chocolate chip pancake in my life. I swear.

Day 3

Dear Diary,
We finally made it to the wax ball factory. But we didn't get to see the wax balls being made. When we were looking at the tub of cooling wax, my dad slipped and did a belly flop into the tub! Ugh!

Day 4

Today we went Wax Ball Bowling. It was pretty fun until Mom's turn. Her finger got stuck in the ball. She went sliding down the lane with it. When she got up, she had a wax bowling pin on her head. Help! Am I related to these people?

Many events have a *cause*—a reason why they happened. The event itself is called the *effect*.

Around the House: Talk with other family members about some funny things that have happened to you or your family. Identify the cause and effect of each thing.

Comprehension

Identify topic, main idea, and supporting details

NAME ____________________

Vote for the President

Help Brad decide who should get his vote for class president. Read this article about the candidates. Write a title for the article. Then circle the main idea in each paragraph. Finally, underline the supporting details. By the time you're finished, you'll probably be able to tell Brad who you think should get his vote.

The *main idea* of a paragraph is what the paragraph is all about. The *supporting details* are the ideas that give support to the main idea.

Great Job. Now cut out this puzzle piece and glue or tape it in the frame on page 64.

NEWS

____

School elections are on Wednesday, and there are three students running for president. Before you decide who to vote for, read about each candidate.

Sam Noodle wants to bring new pastas to our school, including spinach fettucine and pepper linguini. He hopes to serve macaroni and cheese at snack time. Sam also wants to add a weekly cooking class. He hopes to improve the quality of food in our school.

Patricia Cooke (otherwise known as PC) has a real thing for computers. She plans to ask the principal for a new computer for each classroom. PC wants to set up a computer lab for students who want extra computer time. She also hopes to publish a weekly newsletter with computer tips.

Jennie Longshot has already begun a fundraising effort for new sports equipment for the gym. She spoke with the owner of a local sneaker store who says he will give free sneakers to any student who participates in Jennie's jogging class. Jennie wants to help students stay fit. She has even organized daily after-school fitness activities.

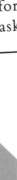

NAME____

Help the Announcers!

It's the day of the big game. Some of the sports announcers are a little confused, though, and the fans are getting restless. If they don't get their acts together soon, it's going to be a madhouse. Read the lines below. Write notes to the announcers to help them correct their mistakes.

The pitch is up by the batter's face. Oooooh! The batter is down. He's holding his eye and yelling. Looks like he's in real pain.

I wonder what's wrong. Do you think a fly went in his eye?

Explain what happened to the batter. ________________________

____

____

____

The batter swings and misses the ball—three strikes and he's out of there. He could have tied the game for the team. Tough luck.

I bet he's going to celebrate with his teammates tonight.

Do you think he's going to be celebrating? Explain your answer.

____

____

____

____

Sometimes we use information we have to figure out things we haven't actually been told. This is called *drawing conclusions*.

NAME ______________________________

Record Breakers

The editors of *The Book of Useless Records* want to create a book of funny records, but they want only facts. Help the editors decide which cards describe facts and which give opinions. Use a red crayon to circle the ones that tell about facts.

A *fact* is something that can be checked by counting, measuring, or checking a reference.

An *opinion* is something that someone thinks or believes, but cannot be proven.

Dear Nutty Editors,
I have the best superball collection in the state of California. I know because my mom told me so. I have so many superballs my mom says we need to give them their own room! My superballs are definitely the coolest.

Superball Bill

Dear Nutty Editors,
I recently entered a bubble blowing contest, and I won! I've enclosed the newspaper article that tells how I blew over 100 bubbles in five minutes. I beat the old record of 98 bubbles.

Chew Gumalot

Dear Nutties,
My cat has lived longer than any cat in the state. She's over 20 years old. She's slowed down a bit but is still an active and happy cat. I've included a copy of her birth certificate as well as an article that appeared in "Pet Parade" last month.

A Proud Owner

Dear Nutty Editors,
I am the nicest person in the world. Everyone tells me I'm nice. No one has ever been mad at me. I've never hurt anyone. Who else in the world can say this? I can, for a fact.

S.O. Nice

Around the House: Work with a family member to find two newspaper articles—one in which the author is presenting facts and another in which the author is presenting an opinion. Which type of article do you prefer to read?

NAME____

It's a Party

Read Alissa's invitation to her birthday party. She's hidden her age within the invitation. Can you figure out how old she's going to be?

Alissa
Sparkle Lane
Gloucester, MA 01930
April 1, 1997

Susie Wynott
Tinsel Street
Salem, MA 01944

Dear Susie,
Please come to my birthday party **N**ext week. **I**t will be on Friday, April 9 at 3:00 PM. The party will be at my house. Call me at home to let me k**N**ow if you will be at the party. My phon**E** number is 283-1234.
I hope to see you at the party!

Sincerely,

Alissa

Alissa will be ____ years old.
Now imagine you're planning your next birthday party. On another sheet of paper, write an invitation to give to your friends. If you want, you can hide a message in the invitation like Alissa did.

Be sure to include the date, time, and place in your invitation. It's also a good idea to give your phone number in an invitation. That way people can call and let you know whether they'll be able to come or not.

NAME ______________________________

Camping Out

Prewriting means you get your ideas down on paper. *Writing* means you write them in full sentences without worrying about grammar or punctuation. *Revising* means you rewrite the story to make sense, and you correct any spelling or grammar errors.

Quentin just returned from a cool camping trip. He wants to write about his trip, but he's having trouble organizing his thoughts. Can you help him organize the information, write a first draft, and revise his story? Follow the directions below.

Step 1: Prewrite

Quentin wrote down a list of ideas. Put checks next to the ones you think he should include in his story.

_______ Swimming in the lake

_______ The car we drove

_______ Climbing the mountain

_______ What happened when the bear came

_______ Setting up the tents

_______ Cleaning up when we got home

Step 2: Write

Now read Quentin's first draft. As you read, think about what he needs to do to improve his story.

Finally when the bear left, we were able to go to sleep. we arrived at camp on a saturday afternoon. As soon as we got there, we set up our tents. The second day, we hiked up a montain. The first day we went swimming in the lake. Swimming made us tired, so we cooked dinner and then got ready to go to sleep. We heard a noise and watched quietly as a bear came of the woods. At the top of the mountain, we build a fire and cooked hot dogs. Our legs were so tired that night that we just laid under the stars and told scary stories. It is a terrific campout!

NAME________________________________

Step 3: Revise

Quentin needs help revising his story. Make marks on the first draft to show him how he might change it to make more sense. Then rewrite the story on the lines below.

Quentin's lucky to have you as his editor! Now, cut out the puzzle piece. Tape or glue it in the puzzle frame on page 64. How's the picture coming?

Around the House: Brainstorm a list of ideas for a story you would like to write. Write a first draft. Then ask a family member to help you revise the story. Rewrite a final copy, and share it with the rest of the family.

NAME ______________________________

Who? What? Where?

A good story has some basic elements: plot, setting, and characters. Read the story Chad wrote below. Then identify the basic elements by filling in the chart on the next page.

Our Sleepover

Last weekend I went to my friend Jonah's house for a sleepover. We ate hot dogs and ice cream, watched a movie and then played some practical jokes on his sister, Eloise. Boy, was she mad! After she went to bed, we stayed up as late as we could, playing video games.

Just when we decided to go to sleep, there was a loud crash and then a raspy sound. Jonah and I looked at each other. We were totally scared. Jonah reached for his baseball bat. "Here, Harry. You take this," he whispered and he handed me a hockey stick.

Jonah led the way down the dark hall to the staircase. We walked downstairs silently. When we got to the bottom, we heard the noise but, this time, it was louder and clearer. It was like a croaking sound, and we both stopped in our tracks.

There was a light coming from the kitchen. I pointed to it and my hand shook like a leaf. Then we saw the shadow, and both of us shrieked and began to run. Jonah suddenly stopped and turned around. Then he began to laugh. "We're so busted!" Jonah said, as he pulled the tablecloth off the kitchen table.

Eloise was sitting there—with a bucket of frogs, laughing as hard as she could! She finally got us back for all the jokes we played on her—worse than we'd ever expected.

The *plot* tells the main events of a story.

NAME____

Plot	Characters	Setting

The *characters* are the people in the story, and the *setting* is when and where the story takes place.

Now, think up some basic elements for your own story. Answer the questions below. Then write your story on another sheet of paper.

1. What is the plot of your story? ____________________

____

____

____

2. Who are the characters?________________________

____

3. What is the setting?____________________________

____

NAME ______________________________

Who Writes What?

Nonfiction books give information that is true and accurate.

Fiction books tell stories or give imaginary information. They are always made up by the author.

Factoid Fred writes nonfiction stories about real people and events. Ronnie the Robot writes fiction stories. Read the descriptions of the books below. Then draw an arrow from each book to the character who is most likely to have written it.

Factoid Fred

Ronnie the Robot

1. This book is about an amazing boy-magician who can turn people into flying creatures.
2. This book is about straw crafts. It tells of more than 100 things you can make from straw.
3. This book is about a pig who saves her farm from an awful, slime-spewing dragon.
4. This book is about a boy known as Ray the Recycler. He has recycled more trash this year than anyone else in Michigan.
5. This book is about the biggest gumball ever made—with pictures and instructions on how to make one of your own.
6. This book is about volcanoes. It tells how they are formed and why they erupt. You will see photographs of the famous Mt. St. Helen's eruption in Washington.

NAME ____

Reading a Poem

It's Reda P. Oem's turn to read a poem aloud, and she's trying to select the one to read. Look at the three choices below. Circle the poem you think Reda should read. Then pretend to be Reda, and practice reading the poem aloud.

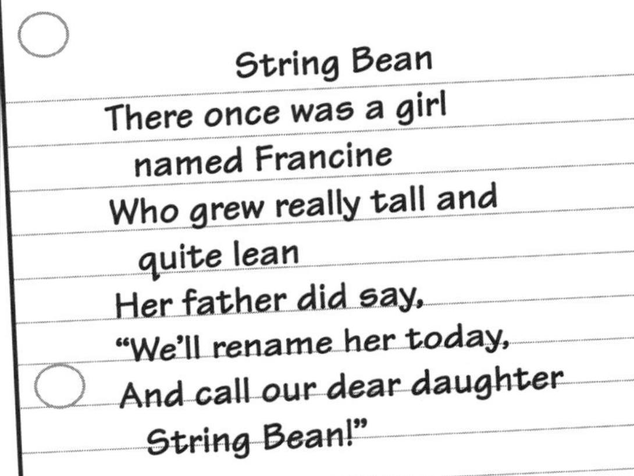

String Bean
There once was a girl
named Francine
Who grew really tall and
quite lean
Her father did say,
"We'll rename her today,
And call our dear daughter
String Bean!"

Spring
Spring, Spring, Spring,
The bird is on the wing.
Now isn't that absurd,
The wing is on the bird.

The Parade
Boom, Boom, Boom
went the band.
The cymbals bang.
The trumpets toot.
The marchers march.
Everyone claps and waves.
Here comes the parade.

After selecting and reading her poem, Reda has to answer some questions about it. Help Reda answer the questions.

1. What is the title of your poem?

   ____

2. Does your poem have rhyming words? ________ If so, list them. ____

3. Are there words in your poem that have interesting sounds? If so, what are they? ______________________

4. Why was this your favorite poem? ______________________

   ____

NAME ________________________________

Writing a Poem

Now Reda needs help writing some poems. Her teacher gave her the incomplete poems below. She is supposed to pick words from the box to fill in the blanks. Help Reda finish the poems.

Poems are shorter than stories. Sometimes they have rhyming words or other special sounds.

morning	lip	tissue	spring
nose	The Sneeze	Achoo	drip
earth	color	wiped	
flowers	watered	red	

A person who writes a poem is called a *poet.*

The Garden

The ____________ were blooming
Green and ____________
Filling the ____________ with ____________ .
Each ____________ the little girl ____________ the plants
So they would bloom all ____________ .

____

" ____________ ," said the boy.
His ____________ it did ____________ .
He reached for a ____________
And ____________ off his ____________ .

Around the House: Poems are fun to read aloud. Ask a family member to listen to the poems you finished on this page. Then try writing a poem of your own.

NAME ______________________________

Dinosaur Days

Ned needs to write a nonfiction article about dinosaurs. Read the paragraph on each book below. If it contains information Ned can use to write his article, circle the paragraph. If it contains information he cannot use, mark an X over it.

Dinosaurs first appeared on Earth 210 million years ago. They were here for 140 million years. Learn about these magnificent creatures in this book.

Dudley was a friend to all dinosaurs. He even had a pet Iguanodon named Iggy. Iggy was a vegesaurus, or plant eater. He was huge, and Dudley liked to take rides on his back.

"There were many different types of dinosaurs," explains Dr. Herrere O. Saurus, a dinosaur scientist. In this fascinating book, learn from Dr. Saurus and other scientists about some of the largest creatures to ever walk the Earth.

Apato was a talking, plant-eating dinosaur who entertained the dinosaur children with wonderful tales about her childhood and life with the other prehistoric creatures. Apato was loved by dinosaurs young and old.

Although no dinosaurs live today, we can learn about them from fossils that are found in the earth. In this book, you can study the photographs of dinosaur fossils that have been discovered around the world.

Did you know that some dinosaurs had magical powers? The Stoneasaurus could turn other creatures into stone by just looking at them. Learn about other mysterious dinosaur powers in this book.

Stories that are true are called *nonfiction*. They are based on real things, events, and people.

Here's your next puzzle piece. Put it in on page 64. You're a puzzle-saurus!

NAME ______________________________

Who's the Librarian?

While at the library, Lewis asked five different people for help finding a biography. He told them what he knew about biographies, and they each suggested a book. The real librarian was the only person who gave Lewis the title of a biography. Read the suggestions each person gave to Lewis. Then write the name of the person you think is the real librarian.

A *biography* tells about someone's life, and it is written by another person.
A *biography* is written about a person who really lives or lived.

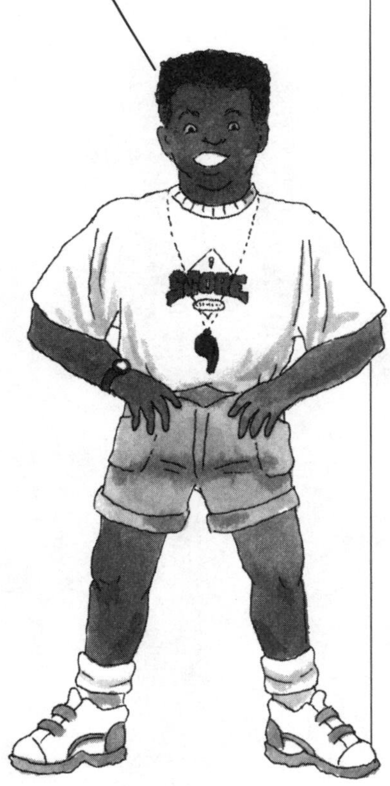

Lewis: A biography tells the story of someone's life.
Mr. Scott: You can read "The Sinking of the Titanic." It's a true story about a ship that sank.

Lewis: A biography tells about one person.
Ms. Ball: I know a book you'll love called "Baseball History." It's about the history of baseball and the famous people that have played it. You'll even learn the rules of the game.

Lewis: A biography is a true story.
Mr. Chaber: You might like "Chuckie Black." It's a cartoon about a boy and his troubles with his talking dog. It's very funny.

Lewis: A biography is usually about a famous or important person.
Ms. Adally: I would suggest "Adventures with Callie." It is a charming book about a girl with superpowers and the adventures she has.

Lewis: A biography is written by someone about someone else.
Mr. Best: You could read the real life story of Bare E. Snuggly, the designer of the Snuggly stuffed bears. You'll learn about his childhood, and how he became successful. The book was written by his son Evan Moore Snuggly.

The real librarian is ____________________.

Around the House: Write the biography of a family member. Talk to the person about his or her life and then write about what they tell you. You might even want to include photographs of the person.

NAME ______________________________

Your Opinion, Please

Movie reviewer Melvin Bigscreen is sick. You have to fill in with a review of the latest box-office hit, *Mission to Mars*. Use information from Melvin's notepad to help you write the review. Start it on the lines below. Finish it on another piece of paper.

Mission to Mars

2 hours of fun	nine-year-old boy goes to Mars
new child actor is great	boy meets space aliens
special effects are unbelievable	spends 2 weeks on Mars
ends on a happy note	brings aliens back to visit his home
very suspenseful	may be scary for very young kids
the jokes are funny	

Mission to Mars

reviewed by ______________________________

____

____

____

____

____

____

At Home: Write a review for a movie you liked. Write about the plot of the movie, why you liked it, and why you think other people would like to see it.

A review tells about a movie, book, or TV show.
It usually tells what the story is about and why the reviewer thinks you would or would not like it.

Grammar and Usage

Identify different kinds of sentences

NAME ______________________________

Nick's Notes

A statement or *declarative sentence* tells something. It ends with a period.

An *interrogative sentence* asks a question. It ends with a question mark. An *exclamatory sentence* shows strong feeling and ends with an exclamation point.

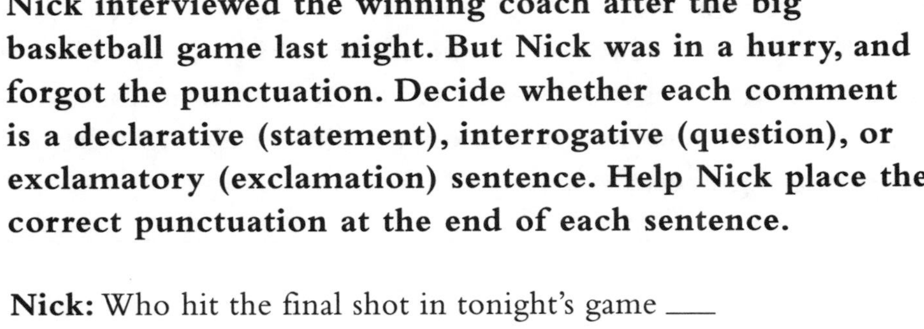

Nick interviewed the winning coach after the big basketball game last night. But Nick was in a hurry, and forgot the punctuation. Decide whether each comment is a declarative (statement), interrogative (question), or exclamatory (exclamation) sentence. Help Nick place the correct punctuation at the end of each sentence.

Nick: Who hit the final shot in tonight's game ___

Coach: Jumpshot Jesse hit a perfect 3-pointer ___

Nick: And who scored the most points ___

Coach: Freddy Finefinger was our high scorer this time ___

Nick: How did the rest of the team play ___

Coach: It was a pretty weak night for the first team ___ Ryan the Rim Man was taken out of the game because of a twisted ankle ___ We really missed him ___ If it hadn't been for Jumpshot and Finefinger, we would definitely have lost the game ___ What a tragedy that would have been ___ We were able to pull it out in the last 3 minutes, though ___

Nick: Wow ___ What an exciting night ___

Coach: You said it ___ And now we're on our way to the finals ___ Will you be attending our game in Denver ___

Nick: I'll be there to cover the BIG WIN ___

Around the House: Listen to a conversation between two people in your family. What kinds of sentences do you hear?

NAME________________________________

Sally's Surprise

Sally found her brother's journal and decided to sneak a peek. It was kind of hard to read because Buddy used a lot of sentence fragments and run-ons. Help Sally read Buddy's entry. Circle the sentence fragments. Underline the run-on sentences. Then rewrite the sentences correctly on the lines below.

Mom and I are planning a great surprise for Sal's birthday we're going to take her to Bongo's Jungle for the whole day. First I'm going. To pretend to have a fight with her. When she gets good and mad. Mom's going to tell her that we have to spend the day at Crazy Aunt Ida's. In the car I'll play the music really loud she'll get so frustrated that she'll put a blanket over her head. When we arrive at Bongo's, she'll look out from under the blanket. And scream. She loves the waterslide and Hippo's Harbor ride. Also loves the foot-long hot dogs and wild berry ice-cream sodas. Mom promised to pay for all the tickets, but I'm going to buy lunch I sure hope Sal is surprised.

A *sentence fragment* does not express a complete thought. *Running in the halls* is a sentence fragment.

A *run-on sentence* is actually two sentences without the correct punctuation and capitalization to separate them. *It was hot we opened the window* is a run-on sentence.

NAME ____

Just the Facts, Please

Sentences are made up of two parts: a subject and a predicate. The *subject* tells who or what the sentence is about. The *predicate* tells the activity in the sentence.

The simple subject is the noun or pronoun that the sentence is about. *Boy, teacher, ocean*, and *house* could all be simple subjects. Simple predicates also refer to just one word—the verb in the sentence. *Runs, is, caught*, and *bakes* can all be simple predicates.

Here are some facts about deserts. Can you simplify each sentence so that all that is left is the simple subject and the simple predicate? Underline the simple subject in each sentence. Circle the simple predicate. Then write the words on the lines below. Unscramble the circled letters to find out where the Great Basin is located.

1. Deserts are very dry areas of land which support very little plant or animal life.
2. People build irrigation canals to channel water into desert areas.
3. In the United States, the Great Basin is the largest desert area.
4. Strong winds form unusual shapes, such as buttes and mesas.
5. The cactus is one of the most familiar plants in the desert.
6. Lizards hide from heat in the desert.

	Subjects	**Predicates**
1.	_ _ _ _ _ ◯ _	_ _ _
2.	_ ◯ _ _ _ _	_ _ _ _ _
3.	_ _ _ _ ◯ _ _ ◯ _ _	_ _
4.	◯ _ _ _ _	_ ◯ _ _
5.	_ _ _ _ ◯ _	_ _
6.	_ _ _ _ _ _ ◯	◯ _ _ _

The Great Basin is located in the

_ _ _ _ _ _ _ _ _ _ .

NAME ______________________________

What's in a Name?

Read the paper Quentin wrote about his summer vacation. Replace each bold-faced common noun with one of the proper nouns in the box below. Cross out the common noun and write the proper noun on the line next to each word.

Jefferson School	Central Park
New York	Arnie Wartznegger
the Empire State Building	Michelle Fife
the Natural History Museum	*Killer Kong*
Aunt Rose	Jamal

I had a terrific summer vacation. My family and I went to visit **my aunt** ______________ in **a city** ______________. She took us everywhere. First, we went to the top of **a building** ______________________________. It was so tall that the people below looked like ants. Then we visited **a museum** ______________________________. It was filled with interesting things. My sister and I especially liked the dinosaur exhibit.

The second day, we spent most of the day in **the park** ______________________. It was a warm and sunny day. We packed a picnic lunch and brought our rollerblades. We also saw some movie actors. **A man** ______________________________ and **a woman** ______________________ were filming **a movie** ______________ near the park. It was very exciting.

I can't wait to get back to **my school** ____________________ to tell **my best friend** ______________ about my trip.

A *noun* names a person, place, or thing.

When a specific person, place, or thing is named, it is called a *proper noun.* A proper noun should always begin with a capital letter.

NAME ______________________________

Spin-a-Noun

Find a friend or family member to play Spin-a-Noun with you. First read the sentences on the gameboard. Underline the subjects in each sentence. Then take turns spinning the spinner. Find a sentence on the gameboard that has a subject that could be replaced by the pronoun you spun. Write the pronoun on the line and put your initials in the square. The first one who gets three squares in a row is the winner.

The words *I, he, she, it, we, you,* and *they* are *pronouns*. They can be used to replace the noun in a sentence when it is the subject.

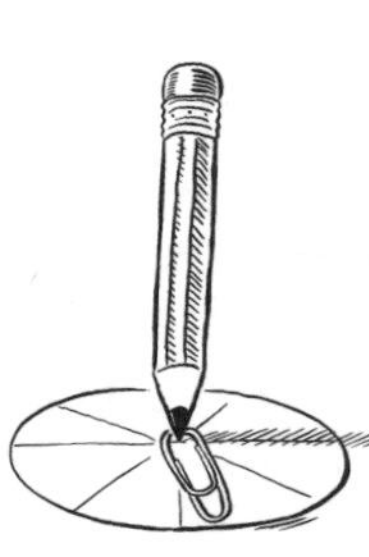

Use a pencil and a paper clip to make a spinner like in the picture. Push the paper clip with your finger to make it spin.

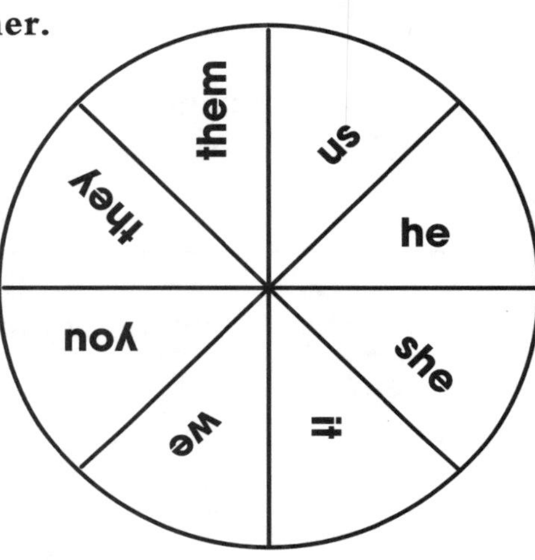

The girls built a treehouse. ______	The lions escaped from the zoo. ______	The carpenter built a house. ______
The waitress dropped the plate. ______	The sun shined brightly. ______	The fireman forgot his boots. ______
The children ran to the field. ______	The books were on the table. ______	Dad wanted his sweater. ______

NAME____

Write the Captions

Frank is creating a photo essay about his trip to the zoo. Look at each picture he took. Then look at the captions he is trying to write. He knows what he wants to say, but is confused about which verb to use. Study his two choices, and circle the correct one.

1. The monkeys (snack, snacks) on bananas.

2. The bear (is resting, are resting) on the rocks.

3. The alligators (smile, smiles) for the camera.

4. The tired baby elephant (sleep, sleeps) in the shade.

5. The zebras (run, runs) from the visitors.

6. The lion (roar, roars) when we get near his cage.

7. The giraffes (is, are) the tallest animals in the zoo.

8. The dolphin (eat, eats) fish out of my hand.

9. The largest gorilla (pound, pounds) his chest proudly.

A *singular noun* usually uses a verb that ends in an *s* or *es*; for example, *Sonya travels* to Spain.
A *plural noun* uses a verb without an *s* or *es*, such as *Sonya and Alicia travel to Italy.*

Grammar and Usage

Use adjectives to add color to a description

NAME ______________________________

Making Sense

Charley Dickens writes for a local magazine. He earns $1 a word for each article he writes. Help Charley earn money by adding as many adjectives as you can to this article. Use the adjectives in the box, or think of some of your own. One is done for you.

An *adjective* is a word used to describe a noun. Adjectives can make a sentence or story more interesting to read.

Adjective Box

~~summer~~	loud	pink	glittery
many	slithering	sweet	long
delicious	plastic	steamy	glowing
fun	shrill	scrumptious	lovely

The Carnival

The ^summer carnival last night was lots of fun. There were rides, food, games, and entertainment.

The Sneaky Snake was my favorite ride. The line was long, but it was worth the wait. When we got into our seats, the music started. The cover came down, and the Snake began to move. Then the seats started shaking. Suddenly the Snake did a double loop, and I heard screams. As soon as the ride was over, almost everyone got back in line.

I tried many things to eat. I enjoyed a candy apple, cotton candy, lemonade, corn on the cob, and a fried chicken leg.

Performers walked around, too. The juggler juggled apples, batons, and sticks. The fire eater swallowed a flame. The musicians played music. All in all, I would say it was a night.

Count your adjectives. How much extra money did Charlie earn? ______________________

Fabulous, outstanding, excellent! You helped Charlie make a fortune. Cut out the puzzle piece on the left now, and glue or tape it in the frame on page 64.

Mechanics

Use correct punctuation for sentences

NAME ______________________________

Pick the Punctuation

Daisy is looking for a job. She's written a letter to an agent to tell about her acting experience. Hopefully, Daisy is a better actress than she is a writer. She's forgotten all the punctuation in her letter. Correct Daisy's letter by adding the punctuation marks where they belong.

Dear TV Agent

I have been acting since I was a young child My first role was in the second grade play I played three different parts I was a snowflake a princess and a tree How's that for real acting My mom thought I was terrific Do you want to call and ask her about my performance

Years later I sang in the Thanksgiving pageant at the mall Wow was it exciting I had the most important part in the pageant I played a turkey running away from a farmer Have you ever heard anyone sing and cluck at the same time

I haven't done much acting since then but I would sure like a chance to work with you You see I'm a natural Are you ready to put me to work

Your friend
Daisy

A *period* is used at the end of a statement. A *question mark* is used at the end of a question. An *exclamation point* is used at the end of an exclamation. *Commas* are used after the opening or closing of a letter, to separate items in a series, or before conjunctions that combine two complete sentences.

Around the House: Check out the punctuation in a letter you've received. Circle the periods, cross out the question marks, and underline the exclamation points.

NAME ______________________________

Capital Idea

Trent works at Trips & Travel Galore. He is helping to create a travel brochure to send to new customers. Look at the pages he has designed so far. He's gotten so excited that he's forgotten all the capital letters. Help Trent fix his brochure by crossing out and rewriting all the letters that should be capitalized.

The first word in a sentence always begins with a capital letter.

You must also capitalize the first letter in all proper nouns.

the united states is full of fun places to visit.

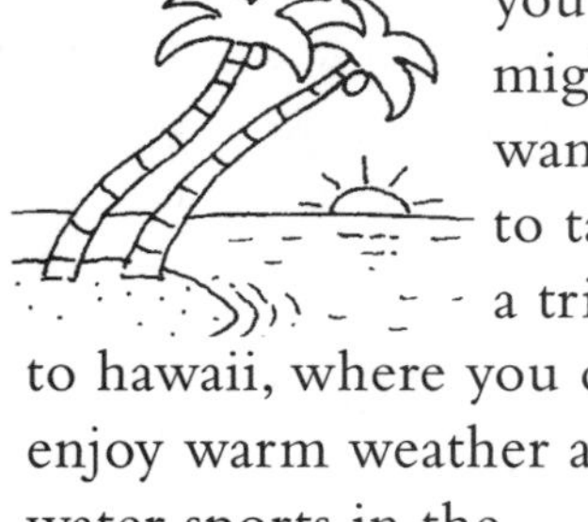

you might want to take a trip to hawaii, where you can enjoy warm weather and water sports in the pacific ocean.

or how about visiting the place where the mississippi river begins? spend some time at lake itasca.

if you like riverboats, you can take a trip down the erie canal on an old barge.

perhaps you'd rather ski in the northeast. Try loon mountain in new hampshire.

let us know where you want to go, and we'll help you get there.

just ask for me, trent travel, at 666-TRIP. if you can't reach me, just speak to my brother travis.

NAME ________________________________

Phonics and Spelling

Identify and use contractions

Contraction Action

Look at the two words on each notecard. Help Contraction Man use his super contraction powers to combine the words to make a contraction. Write the contraction on the line. If the words cannot be combined to form a contraction, mark an X over the notecard. The first one is done for you.

When two words are combined, and letters are left out and replaced with an apostrophe, the new word is called a *contraction*. Some examples are:

cannot → can't
are not → aren't
we will → we'll

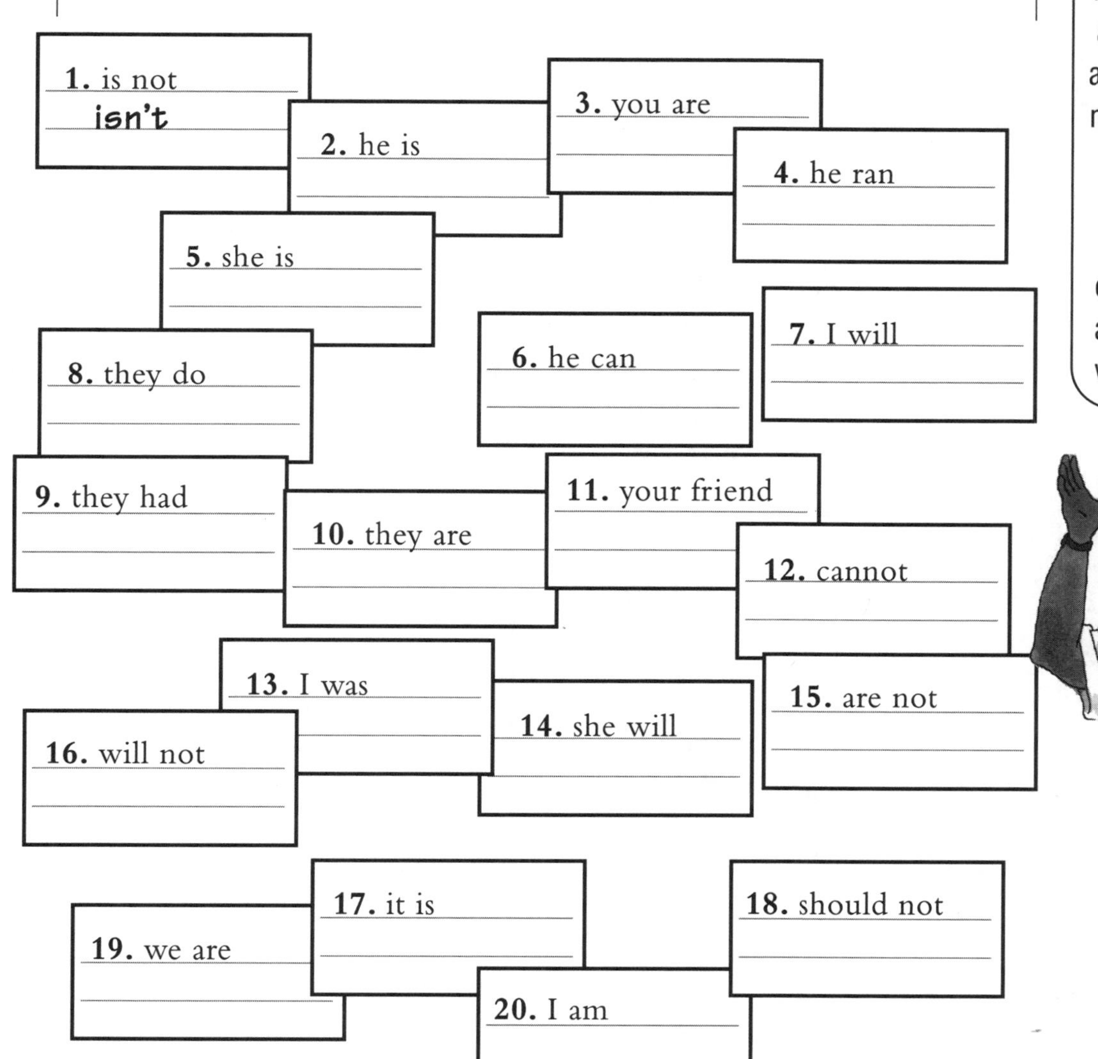

1. is not
isn't
2. he is
3. you are
4. he ran
5. she is
6. he can
7. I will
8. they do
9. they had
10. they are
11. your friend
12. cannot
13. I was
14. she will
15. are not
16. will not
17. it is
18. should not
19. we are
20. I am

Vocabulary

Identify and use homonyms

NAME ________________________________

Fran's Photos

Homonyms are words that sound the same and are spelled the same, but they have different meanings. Look at the homonyms in these sentences.

The baby watched the **top** as it spun.

Put the **top** back on the jar.

Fran took some great photographs last summer. These six are especially interesting because they can each be described by using a pair of homonyms. Look at the homonym pairs in the box. Write a sentence to describe each picture using a different homonym pair. We've done one to help you get started.

bat bat	~~fair fair~~	park park	block block

It wasn't fair that the fair was closed when we arrived.

____

____

____

NAME________________________________

New Words

A *prefix* is a word part that is added to the beginning of a base word. A *suffix* is a word part that is added to the ending of a base word.

These word parts can change the meaning of a base word. For example, friend can be changed to unfriendly.

Take turns playing a word game with a friend. Make as many words as you can by using the base words, prefixes, and suffixes below. Write the new words on the lines. Give yourself 1 point for each word that uses one prefix or suffix. Give yourself 3 points for each word that uses one prefix and one suffix. See who has the most points after a set period of time.

Prefix	Base Word		Suffix
un	do	happy	ly
re	view	cook	able
pre	make	cut	ment
	safe	wind	ing

Take a look at this puzzle piece and glue or tape it in place on page 64.

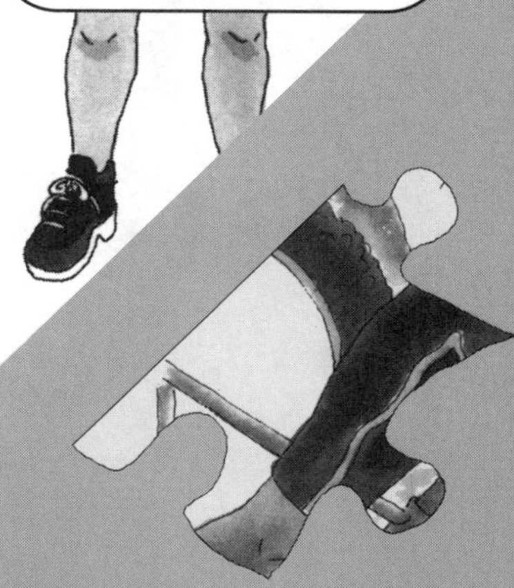

Around the House: Look with family members through magazines, newspapers, or catalogs to find examples of words with prefixes and suffixes. Can you identify the base word in each one?

NAME ____________________

Shirts for Sale

An *idiom* is a figure of speech. It is a phrase or sentence that doesn't mean exactly what it sounds like it means.

For example, if I say *"Hold your horses,"* I am not expecting you to find some horses to hold onto. That idiom means to stop what you're doing or slow down.

Shari the shirtmaker makes shirts with idioms on them. She's made four new shirts today. Each customer below wants to buy one. Read the sentences on the shirts and think about what the boldfaced words mean. Then match each shirt with the person who should buy it. Write the number of the shirt in the blank on that person's T-shirt.

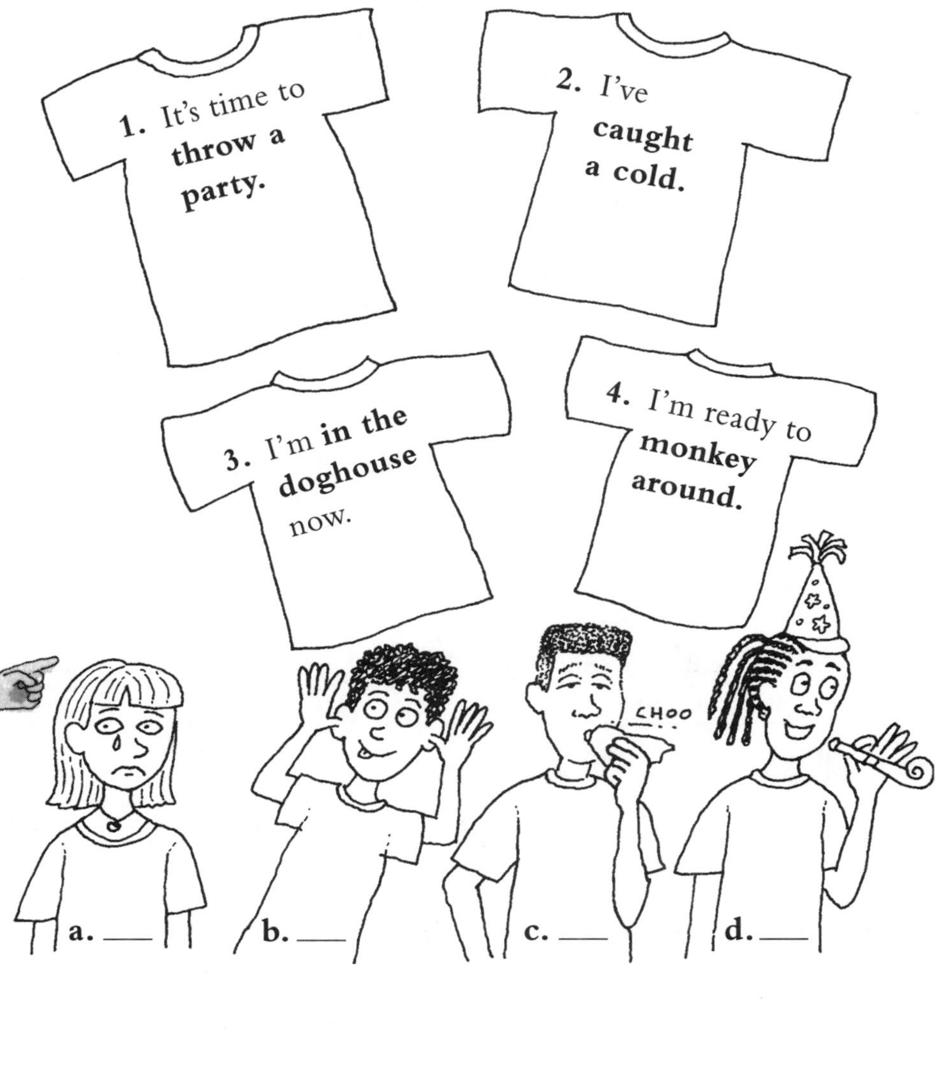
1. It's time to **throw a party.**
2. I've **caught a cold.**
3. I'm **in the doghouse** now.
4. I'm ready to **monkey around.**
CHOO
a. ___
b. ___
c. ___
d. ___

NAME ______________________________

A Family Favorite

Carol found this recipe in a cookbook in her grandmother's attic, but some of the words have faded over the years. Read each sentence carefully. Use context clues to decide what word used to be in each blank. Write that word on the line.

Follow these 10 easy steps to make a tasty snack.

1. Preheat the __________ to 375°.
2. Use your bare __________ to butter a pan.
3. Use a __________________ to measure 2 cups of flour, 1 cup of sugar, and $\frac{1}{2}$ cup of milk.
4. Pour all of these ingredients into a large metal __________.
5. Use a knife to__________the butter into small pieces.
6. Add the butter, and then stir everything together with a __________ until smooth.
7. Add small pieces of chocolate__________ to the batter.
8. Put blobs of batter onto the buttered __________. You should be able to make about 24 __________.
9. Cook for only a few __________ —nine at the most. Bake until golden brown.
10. When they are cool, eat your __________with milk.

Draw a picture of what this old family recipe is for.

Vocabulary

Use figurative language

NAME ______________________________

Simile Sentences

Read the descriptions below. Choose a simile from the box to complete each description. Write it on the line. We've done the first one for you.

quiet as a mouse	~~sings like a bird~~	eats like a horse
hard as a rock	white as snow	swims like a fish

A *simile* uses *like* or *as* to compare two things. For example, you might say, "I'm as hungry as a bear."

You're as sharp as a tack! Now cut out this puzzle piece and tape or glue it in place on page 64.

1. My brother is a great singer. He has a really nice voice. Everyone likes to hear him sing because it sounds so pretty. He sings like a bird ______________________.

2. My young cousin can already swim all the way across the pool. She is really becoming a good swimmer. She ______________________.

3. I left my playdough out all night last night. It is so hard now that I can't even mold it. It feels solid and firm. It's as ______________________.

4. Craig eats all the time. Right after dinner, he always makes another snack. If he opens the chips, he eats the whole bag. He just eats and eats and eats. He ______________________.

5. When my baby brother is asleep, everyone in our house has to be very quiet. Mom gets mad if a door slams or a book drops. She wants me to be as ______________________.

6. We just got a new puppy and she is white. Her fur is a pure, bright white, and there are no hints of gray or black anywhere. She is as ______________________.

NAME ____

Fun with Words

Try to say this tongue twister three times very quickly:

Shelly shared a strawberry shake with Sam.

Write some tongue twisters of your own by completing the sentences below. Then copy them on slips of paper, and pass them out to friends and family members. Have them try to say the tongue twisters as many times as they can.

1. Cheerful Charlie chose a chocolate ch ______________.
2. Please pass the p ______________ p ______________.
3. Three thick thieves th ______________ th ______________.
4. Sweet Sally Sue s______________ s______________.
5. Four fine fresh f______________ f______________f______________.
6. Wiggly worms w______________ w______________.

Another way to have fun with sentences is to use onomatopoeia. Choose a word that uses onomatopoeia and write it in a blank to complete each sentence.

hissed	growled
buzzed	popped

7. The bee ______________ by my ear.
8. When the tea kettle______________, I knew the water was hot.
9. I was so hungry my stomach ______________.
10. The popcorn crackled as it ______________.

Alliteration is when you use words with the same beginning sounds in a sentence. The reason tongue twisters are a challenge is because they use alliteration. *Onomatopoeia* refers to words that sound like what they mean; for example, *roar, boom,* and *bang.*

NAME ____________________

Can You Compare?

Analogies compare things. Look at this analogy:

***Big* is to *little* as *up* is to *down*.**

The first words being compared are big and little. Since these words are opposites, up and down must be opposites also.

Read each sentence and decide how to complete the analogy. Circle the letter in front of the word you choose. Then write the letters in order on the lines to finish the sentence below. The first one is done for you.

Look carefully at the first two things being compared and think about how they are related. Then choose a word that will give the next two things the same kind of relationship.

1.	Car is to road as train is to	(C.) track	B. sky
2.	Nest is to bird as a shell is to	A. beach	O. turtle
3.	Hat is to head as glove is to	A. snow	M. hand
4.	Flute is to music as paintbrush is to	P. art	M. paints
5.	Red is to apple as green is to	A. grass	A. animal
6.	Whale is to ocean as bird is to	R. sky	B. flying
7.	Bank is to money as refrigerator is to	A. ice	I. food
8.	Teacher is to school as sailor is to	S. boat	B. hotel
9.	Electricity is to radio as food is to	O. people	B. refrigerator
10.	Doorknob is to door as clasp is to	A. key	N. necklace
11.	Person is to run as horse is to	S. gallop	B. jump

YOU MADE C __ __ __ __ __ __ __ __ __ __ !

NAME____

What's the Point?

Maggie A. Zine is an editor for *Kids Only Magazine*. Read the descriptions of the articles and games planned for next month's issue. Help Maggie decide what the purpose of each one is. Write I for Inform, P for Persuade, or E for Entertain on the line.

Kids Only Magazine

No More Broccoli: Joan Nobroc explains why all kids should join her boycott of the hated vegetable. __________

The A, B, C's of Best Friends: Learn all you need to know about becoming a great best friend. __________

Celebrity Braces: Do you know how many celebrities have worn braces? Look at the photos, and then find the names of these famous stars in the word search. __________

Paper Clips Rule: Ima Clipmeister tells why the new paper clip collecting craze is totally cool, and why you should collect clips, too.

____

101 Uses for Chewed Gum: You can do more with your chewed gum than stick it under desks and chairs. Make necklaces, hang pictures, wrap presents, and much, much more. __________

Perfect Pet-People Dos: Check out these illustrations of matching hairdos for pets and their owners. __________

Check Yourself: Does Maggie have a variety in the types of features planned for this issue? Put the letters you wrote in the boxes column by column. Do you have two PIEs in a row?

☐ ☐ ☐ ☐ ☐ ☐

If you think the purpose of the article is to give you information about something, write I for *Inform*. If it sounds like the author is trying to get you to do something, write P for *Persuade*. If the article just sounds like it's supposed to be fun, write E for *Entertain*.

NAME ______________________________

Help Henrietta

Henrietta's father wrote directions for her to walk home from school. Read the directions, and then draw a line on the map to show the path Henrietta should take. Then answer the questions below.

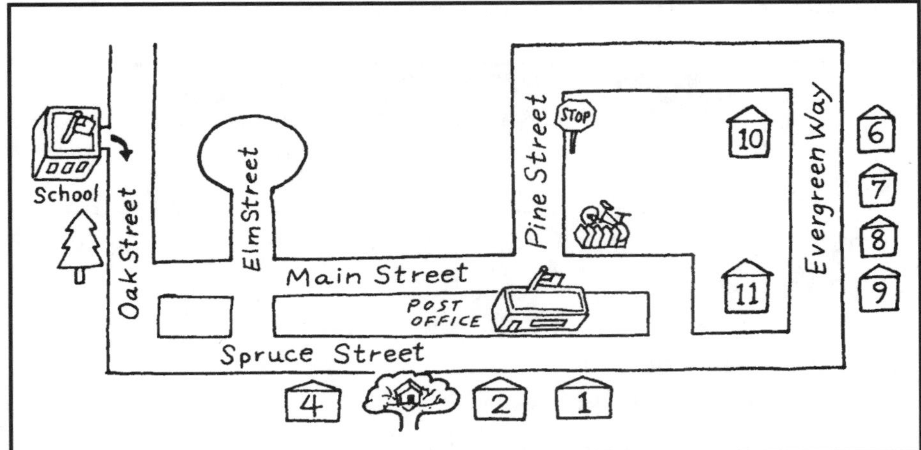

Directions: Walk down Oak St. until you get to the large pine tree. Turn left onto Main St. Walk about halfway down Main St. Turn left at the post office. The bicycle racks should be on your right. Keep walking straight until you get to the stop sign. Turn right. At the end of the street turn right again. Our house is the third one on the left.

1. What number house does Henny live in? ______________

Now Henny wants to visit her friend Sarah. Follow these directions to get to Sarah's house.

From the front steps of the house, take a left. Walk to the end of the street. Take a right turn. Walk straight. Sarah lives one house after the tree house.

2. What number house does Sarah live in? ______________

Check Yourself: Henny's house number is twice as large as Sarah's house number.

When you follow directions, it's important to follow them one step at a time, in the order they are written.

NAME ______________________________

A Day in Your Life

It happened so quickly that you can hardly believe it, but you are now the most famous child in America. All the magazines and television stations are begging you for an interview. So you've decided to write a personal narrative about a typical day in your life. You plan to give it to all the news organizations, and then you're hoping to be left alone! To get started, answer the questions below.

1. What things do you do in the morning when you wake up?

____

____

2. What time do you leave for school? How do you get there?

____

3. What are some of the things you do in school? ______________

____

4. What do you do after school? Do you have after school activities? Do you have friends you play with? ______________

____

____

5. What do you do in the evenings? Do you eat dinner with your family? Do you read? Do you watch TV? Do you ride your bike or take walks? ______________

____

____

Now use the information in your answers to write a narrative about a day in your life. Add other ideas if you want to. Write your narrative on another sheet of paper.

A *personal narrative* tells about you and the things you do. The most important thing about a personal narrative is that it is written by *you*.

Cut out the puzzle piece and decide where it goes on page 64. Glue or tape it in place.

NAME ______________________________

It's a Match

In this game, you must match a topic sentence with the detail sentences that support it. First make 16 paper rectangles that are the same size as the ones below. Put a rectangle over each box on both pages. Then uncover one box on each page. If the two boxes have information that could be put together to form a paragraph, you have a match.

A *topic sentence* tells what a paragraph is about.

The *detail sentences* give details that support the topic sentence.

1. I learned a lot at camp.	**5.** Cats are the best pets.
2. Today I made breakfast.	**6.** I saw the silliest movie.
3. I like reading books.	**7.** Fruits are good for you.
4. My favorite sport is soccer.	**8.** Yesterday I went bike riding with a friend.

NAME______________________________

Give yourself two points for every match. If the boxes don't match, cover them again and let your opponent take a turn. When all the boxes have been uncovered, the player with the most points wins.

a. I made blueberry pancakes and covered them with maple syrup. I also made hot chocolate with milk and melted marshmallow. It was delicious.	**e.** They love to cuddle up in your lap. You know when they're happy because they purr. And, you don't need to take cats for walks.
b. These naturally sweet foods have lots of vitamins and nutrients. They help our bodies grow and stay strong. They also give us lots of energy to play.	**f.** When I read, I'm able to visit far-off places in my mind. I get to meet interesting characters, both real and make-believe.
c. I learned how to swim and play softball. I also learned how to make friendship bracelets and sing new songs.	**g.** You get to play outside with a group of friends. You get to kick a ball and run really fast. You can even hit the ball with your head. Now that's a fun sport.
d. We met at my house and rode straight to the park. We followed the trails there for almost two hours. Most of the ride was fun, but biking up the big hill was really hard.	**h.** It was about a dog who left home by mistake. Dognappers try to steal her. Every time they catch her, they make a mistake, and the dog gets away.

Good game. Now, cut out the puzzle piece. Go to the puzzle frame on page 64. Decide where it fits, and tape or glue it in place.

Around the House: Look at newspapers and magazines you have at home. See if you can identify the topic sentences and the detail sentences.

NAME ____________________

A Nose for News

Nancy writes for her neighborhood newsletter. She has to look over a new writer's article to make sure it is well-written and informative. Help Nancy fill in the chart to make sure the article gives all the necessary information.

NEWS

Million Dollar Day at the Beach

Nina and Mark Glass found an incredible treasure at Sands Point Beach yesterday afternoon. They were building a sandcastle for the annual sand sculpture contest when Nina suddenly spotted something shiny in the sand. It was a beautiful clear stone, so she immediately picked it up and placed it on the tower of her sand castle.

After the contest, Nina and Mark brought the stone to the police station in Sands Point. The sergeant on duty took it to a jeweler who thinks that the stone is a 3-carat diamond. He believes it probably fell out of someone's ring. If the diamond is not claimed by next Friday, the Glass children will be allowed to keep it. They are planning to give it to their mother for her birthday.

Who? ____________________

What? ____________________

When? ____________________

Where? ____________________

Why? ____________________

How? ____________________

NAME ____

Now write a news story about something that has happened in your neighborhood or at your school recently. Be sure your story answer the six important questions—Who, What, When, Where, Why, and How. Begin your story here. Use another sheet of paper to finish it.

____

____

____

____

____

____

____

____

____

____

____

____

____

____

____

All news stories should answer six questions.
They are who, what, when, where, why, and how—5 W's and an H.

Around the House: Get a copy of your local newspaper, and pick one story. Have a 5 W's and H Hunt with a family member. How quickly can you find the who, what, when, where, why, and how of the story?

Written Expression

Conduct and write an interview

NAME ______________________________

Interviewing

Felicia's class is learning to conduct interviews. Their teacher taught them to take careful notes when interviewing people. Study the notes Felicia took when she interviewed her Aunt Gert. Then look at the story she wrote about her.

When you write about a person, you can show that you talked to that person by using direct quotes. That means that in some of your sentences you tell the exact words the person said about a particular subject.

Notes

1. favorite games–hopscotch, leapfrog, pin the tail on the donkey
2. favorite sports–always played basketball with brothers, proudest of being the fastest runner in 4th grade class
3. favorite food–bubble gum ice-cream, pickles, homemade lemonade, my dad's famous hot dog stew
4. favorite subject in school–recess, of course, was all-time favorite, but liked science, too, always interested in bugs

My Interview With Aunt Gert

When Aunt Gert came to visit last summer, I asked her about some of her favorite things. Aunt Gert quickly answered, "I loved hopscotch, leap frog, and pin the tail on the donkey."

Then I asked about sports, and Aunt Gert replied, "I played basketball with my brothers, but my greatest accomplishment was being the fastest runner in fourth grade."

Aunt Gert was happy to tell me about her favorite foods. She said, "I like bubble-gum ice cream, pickles, lemonade, and my daddy's famous hot-dog stew."

I ended the interview by asking Aunt Gert about her favorite subject in school. She responded quickly, "Recess, of course, was my all-time favorite, but I liked science, too. I was always interested in bugs."

NAME ____________________

Now conduct your own interview with a family member about his or her favorite things. Take notes or record the interview with a video or tape recorder. Then write about your interview using dialogue. Let everyone in your family read it.

Put the quotation marks before the first word the person said and after the punctuation; for example, My dad said, "When I was a kid, my favorite sport was basketball."

What an interview! Cut out the puzzle piece on the left and tape or glue it in place on page 64.

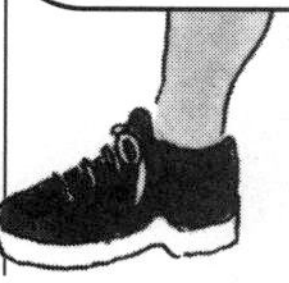

NAME ______________________________

Write it, Read it

Look at the pictures of Beth and Christina's day. Beneath each picture, write what you think is happening. Then use your notes to write a story about their day. Use another sheet of paper if you need to, and add as many details as you want.

A *story* tells about events in the order that they happened. When you finish writing a story, you should always read it again to make sure it makes sense. Check it for grammar and spelling mistakes.

____
____
____

____
____
____

____
____
____

____
____
____

NAME______________________________

Fairy Tale Fun

What are some of the things you find in fairy tales? Think about stories such as *Cinderella, Aladdin,* and *The Little Mermaid*. Check off the things that are familiar.

____ **1.** Fairy tales often start with: *Once upon a time…*

____ **2.** Witches sometimes cast spells.

____ **3.** There are always natural disasters.

____ **4.** The characters are unhappy at the beginning and unhappy at the end.

____ **5.** There are usually magical fairies or wizards.

____ **6.** Characters often have to do something by a certain time.

____ **7.** You learn about the characters from the time they are born to old age.

____ **8.** Characters often fall in love and live happily ever after.

Use what you remember from fairy tales you've read and from the list above to write your own fairy tale. Begin your story here. Continue it on another piece of paper.

____

____

____

____

____

____

____

____

____

It's no tale that you've written a great fairy tale. Take this puzzle piece and place it in the frame on page 64. Try to guess what the picture is going to be.

Grammar and Usage

Combine sentences with commas and conjunctions

NAME ________________________________

But, Coach...

A *conjunction* is used to connect two sentences. Common conjunctions are *and, but, so,* and *or.*

When using a conjunction to combine two complete sentences, you must put a comma before the conjunction.

Edna is trying to explain why she missed tennis practice. Read Edna's excuses. Choose the correct conjunction *and, or, but,* or *so* to combine each pair of sentences. Then write the new sentence on the line.

1. I didn't mean to miss practice. It just couldn't be helped.

____

2. After school today, I was really hungry. I went to get a snack.

____

3. When I finished my snack, I realized I didn't have my sneakers. I didn't know where they were. ________________________________

4. I looked everywhere. I couldn't find them. ________________________________

5. I went straight to the phone. I called my mom.________________________________

6. She said she could bring me another pair of sneakers. She could help me find my old ones. ________________________________

NAME ______________________________

Camp News

JoJo wrote this letter on the first day of camp and never mailed it. It is now the last day, and everything she wrote about has already happened. Can you help her rewrite the letter? Cross out the present and future tense verbs. Write the correct past tense verb above them. One has been done for you.

Dear Mom,

Summer camp ~~is~~ was so much fun. Sunday night is the annual Water Balloon War. I'm the captain of the Tornadoes this year. The other team is the Hurricanes.

Monday morning is the big swim competition. We have the best swimmer, Frank E. Fish, on our team. Monday afternoon we will practice our songs for that night's singing competition. After the show, it will be time for the jello-eating contest. I think I'll win.

Tuesday is the day for soccer games, volleyball games, and relay races. That night the judges will announce the winning team.

Thanks for letting me come to camp again, Mom. It looks like it's going to be the best year ever!

Love,

JoJo

Verbs tell what is happening and when it happens.

Each of these sentences tell about the same event happening at a different time.

Ben *jumps* to catch the ball. (present tense, happening now)

Ben *jumped* to catch the ball. (past tense, already happened)

Ben *will jump* to catch the ball. (future tense, will happen in the future)

Grammar and Usage

Use adverbs correctly

NAME ______________________________

Add the Adverb

Adverbs are used to modify or describe verbs. Many adverbs end with the letters *ly*.
Adverbs often come just before or after the verb they are modifying.

Ian loves to tell about the time he went fishing with his Great Uncle Dave. Although the fishing trip was a success, Ian's description isn't quite right. Help Ian fix his sentences. Rewrite each one, moving the underlined adverb to the place in the sentence where it makes sense.

1. I missed Uncle Dave's <u>nearly</u> phone call when he invited me to go fishing. ______________________________

____

2. I gathered my <u>quickly</u> rod, hook, and bait. ______________________________

____

3. I ran down to the <u>happily</u> pond. ______________________________

____

4. Uncle Dave was waiting with his <u>already</u> equipment.

____

5. We baited our <u>successfully</u> hooks and dropped our lines into the water. ______________________________

____

6. My <u>slowly</u> line started to quiver. ______________________________

____

7. Then <u>strongly</u> it shook. ______________________________

____

8. Uncle Dave helped <u>finally</u> me steady it. ______________________________

____

9. I had caught a huge fish which we ate for <u>gladly</u> dinner.

____

NAME ______________________________

Find the Owners

Look at the items in the Lost and Found. Then look at the list on the left that tells who owns each item. On the line next to each item, write a possessive phrase to show who owns each one. The first one is done for you.

The book belongs to John.

The cap belongs to Marcia.

The football belongs to the 5th grade boys.

The purse belongs to my teacher.

The glasses belong to Ms. Jackson.

The whistles belong to the coaches.

The briefcase belongs to our principal.

Possessive nouns show that something belongs to something or someone else. *The boy's bicycle* means the bicycle belongs to the boy.

We usually add *'s* to make words possessive. If an *s* has already been added to show that a word is plural, just add an ' after the s.

Mechanics

Use basic abbreviations

NAME ______________________________

Abbreviation Hunt

Abbreviations are shortened forms of some commonly used words. How often do you think abbreviations are used in writing? Play a game with a friend or family member to find out.

Abbreviations are shortened forms of common words. Most abbreviations end with a period.

Mrs. and *Mr.* are abbreviations for Misses and Mister.

Here's how:

1. Gather books, magazines, and newspapers.
2. Cut out twenty small cards. On each card, write one of the following words:

Mister	Street	foot
Misses	pound	yard
Doctor	Avenue	United States of America
Senator	inch	President
road	Street	etcetera
Television	representative	corporation
Farenheit	Celsius	

3. Mix the cards up, and turn them face down on a table.
4. Take turns flipping over one card at a time. Look at the word on the card, and decide what the abbreviation is for that word. Then take 2 minutes to find an example of that abbreviation in a book, magazine, or newspaper. If you find it, show it to your opponent, and keep the card. If not, turn the card back over.
5. The game is over when all the cards have been used. The player with the most cards wins.

You're quite a hunter! Good Job. Now cut out this puzzle piece, and "hunt" for its place in the frame on page 64. Glue or tape it in place.

GO!

Around the House: Look at a piece of mail addressed to someone in your home. How many abbreviations can you find? Try to write the address without any abbreviations.

NAME ______________________________

What Comes First?

Chad needs to use the encyclopedia to look up the topics listed in the left column. He could find his topics more quickly if they were in alphabetical order. Rewrite the topics in alphabetical order on the lines. Then write the letters for the volume in which Chad would find each topic.

To put words in alphabetical order, look at the first letter. The words that begin with A go first, then the words that begin with B, then the words that begin with C, etc.

If two words begin with the same letter, go to the second letter. If the second letter is the same, go to the third letter, and so on.

Crocodiles ______________ Vol. ______

Planets ______________ Vol. ______

Environment ______________ Vol. ______

Water ______________ Vol. ______

Plants ______________ Vol. ______

Armadillos ______________ Vol. ______

Soils ______________ Vol. ______

Ocean Life ______________ Vol. ______

Rivers ______________ Vol. ______

Tornadoes ______________ Vol. ______

Earthquakes ______________ Vol. ______

Volcanoes ______________ Vol. ______

Computers ______________ Vol. ______

Bridges ______________ Vol. ______

Machines ______________ Vol. ______

Cameras ______________ Vol. ______

NAME ______________________________

Quentin's Questions

Quentin is always full of questions. His mother wants to find the answers, but sometimes she's not sure where to look. Study the questions Quentin is asking. Decide which resource his mother should use to find the answer to each question. Write the first letter of that resource on the line below Quentin's question.

An *encyclopedia* gives a lot of information about a subject. A *dictionary* tells the meaning of a word and how to pronounce it.

A *thesaurus* lists synonyms and words that are similar in meaning to a word, and an *atlas* is a book of maps.

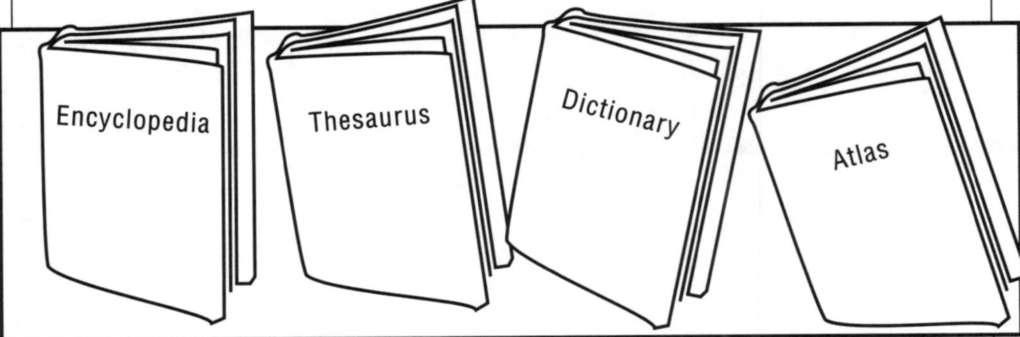

1. What does *hinder* mean? ______

2. Can you think of a word that means the same thing as *special?* ______

3. When do snakes shed their skin? ______

4. What is the longest river in the United States? ______

5. What is the largest country in North America? ______

6. How do you spell *industrial?* ______

7. What are some more interesting words for my story? ______

8. Who invented the first car? ______

NAME ____

Karl's Custard

Jeanine wants to make her brother Karl's favorite dessert, banana-fudge swirl custard with blueberry frosting. She has her mom's dessert cookbook, but she needs help finding the recipe.

Now you're cookin'! Put this puzzle piece in place on page 64 and you're almost done.

1. Now Jeanine looks at the book's Table of Contents. Circle the entries in which Jeanine might find the recipe.

Table of Contents

Chocolate Cakes	pages 1–8
Coffee Cakes	pages 8–15
Cookies	pages 16–24
Custards and Creams	pages 25–29
Frostings	pages 30–40
Fruit Desserts	pages 40–55

2. Jeanine looks up a few entries but she just gets more confused. Then she remembers the index at the back of the book. Here are a few listings from the index. On what pages should Jeanine look to find the recipe? ______________________

cookies, peanut butter	page 24
custard, banana-fudge swirl	page 27
custard, coconut cream	page 29
frosting, blueberry	page 30
frosting, vanilla	page 40

4. Jeanine made an awesome custard. Now she wants to find more books with dessert recipes. Circle the books that might give her some ideas.

a. Jules Children, *Meats and Poultry*, Boston, MA, Cooks Press 1997

b. Jules Children, *Sweets are Neat!,* Boston, MA, Cooks Press 1997

c. Jeff Jones, *Lotsa Sausage,* Chicago, IL, Chef Inc. 1994

NAME ______________________________

Dictionary Definitions

Wanda Wordsworth loves words. She has zillions of dictionaries because she enjoys looking up words. Today she is looking up words that begin with the letter S. Here's a page from Wanda's dictionary. Read it carefully, and then answers the questions below.

A *dictionary* is a reference book that lists words in alphabetical order. It gives the meaning, pronunciation, part of speech, and other information about each word.

shooting star **Shoshone**

shooting star *n* A briefly visible meteor.
shop (shop) *n* **1.** A small retail store. **2.** A place where goods are manufactured. **3.** A commercial or industrial establishment. **4.** A workshop—*v* shopped, shopping, To visit stores to inspect and buy merchandise.
short•cake (shôrt´-kāk) *n* A cake made with rich dough, split and filled with fruit.
short•stop (shôrt´-stop) *n* *Baseball.* **1.** The field position between second and third bases. **2.** The player who occupies this position.
short•tempered (short´-tem-pard) *adj* Easily angered.
Sho•sho•ne (shə-shōń-ē) *n, pl* **-ne** or**-nes**. Also **Sho•sho•ni** *pl.* **-ni** or **-nis.** **1. a.** A tribe of Indians, formerly occupying parts of the western United States. **b.** A member of this tribe. **2.** The Uto-Aztecan language of the Shoshone.

1. What are the guide words on this page? ______________________

2. What is a shooting star? ______________________

3. How do you pronounce the word *Shoshone?* ______________________

4. Use the word *short-tempered* in a sentence. ______________________

____

____

____

NAME ________________________________

The Bullfighter

Bev has always been interested in bullfighting. Take a look at this encyclopedia entry she found. Then answer the questions at the bottom of the page.

Encyclopedia of the World
1996 Edition

DABULL, I. BEATO (born 1962). In 1980, I. Beato Dabull began attending Matador University, where he learned to twirl his cape, yell *charge*, and run away from a bull without getting hurt. His distinguished career began at the Worldwide Bullfighter's Challenge in 1983. Dabull has been in the ring with more than 300 bulls. He was voted best matador in the Bullfighting Tournaments of 1993, 1994, and 1995. Dabull is also a matador instructor and has taught thousands of young people the secrets of his success.
Other related articles: Bullfighting, MVP Bullfighters, Bullfighting Tournaments.

1. To find this entry about I. Beato Dabull, Bev must have looked in which encyclopedia?

A. **B** B. **D** C. **I**

2. Would this entry have any information about I. Beato Dabull's career in 1997? Why or why not? ________

____
____
____

3. How old was Dabull when his career began? ________

4. Name three other articles that might have information about I. Beato Dabull.

____
____
____
____
____
____
____

An *encyclopedia* is a set of reference book with articles on many different subjects
The articles are listed in alphabetical order, and they give detailed information about their subjects.

NAME ________________________________

Daisy's Dog Bones

Daisy the Dalmation loves her Dog Bone Snacks. She was eating so many that her owner, Delilah, decided to make a graph to keep track of Daisy's snacking. Use the bar graph to answer some questions about Daisy and the dog bones she eats.

To find out how many dog bones Daisy had in a day, find that day of the week.

Then look at the bones above that day. Go to the top of the bone, and run your finger across the graph to the number that the top of the pile is even with.

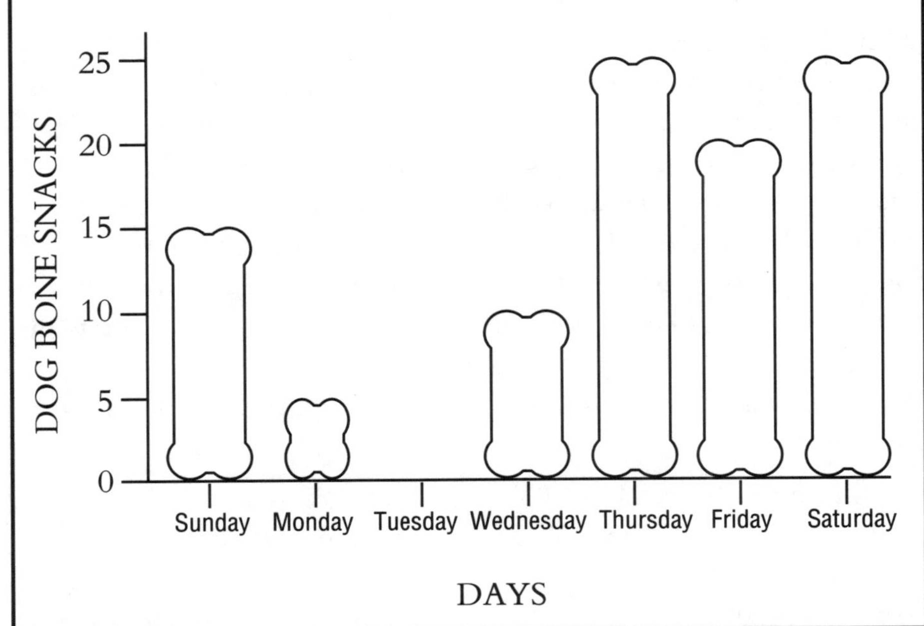

1. How many Dog Bone Snacks did Daisy eat all week?

____

2. On which day did she eat the fewest snacks? ____________

On which days did she eat the most snacks? ____________

3. Did she eat more dog bone snacks in the beginning of the week or at the end? ____________

4. Did Daisy eat more dog bones on Friday or Saturday? ________

________ How many more? ________

NAME ______________________________

Widge-Pidget Jrs.

Betty's writing a report on Widge-Pidget Jrs. She needs to find out what they are, what they are made from, and what they do. Read the information about Widge-Pidget Jrs. Then take some notes to help Betty with her report.

Widge-Pidget Jrs. are small, sticky shapes created by inventor Samuel Widge-Pidget (born 1945). In July 1993 some sticky stuff dripped into a circular cookie cutter. The sticky stuff hardened into a flat circle. Widge-Pidget discovered that it was very sticky and strong. But it wasn't messy like glue! This got him thinking about the uses for the sticky circle.

He decided to make more circles. He put these sticky circles all over a wall, hanging his clothes and shoes on them. No sticky stuff got on his clothes or shoes! Widge-Pidget found that his sticky shapes could be used to hang signs and even books on the wall. They could also be used as decorations. Now he sells millions of these sticky shapes each year.

Use the space below to take notes. Write the information about Widge-Pidget Jrs. that you think is most important.

____

____

____

____

____

____

____

____

____

To take notes on what you read, write just enough to help you remember the information you need.
Superb note-taking! Now cut out the puzzle piece and glue or tape it in the correct place on page 64. What have you made?

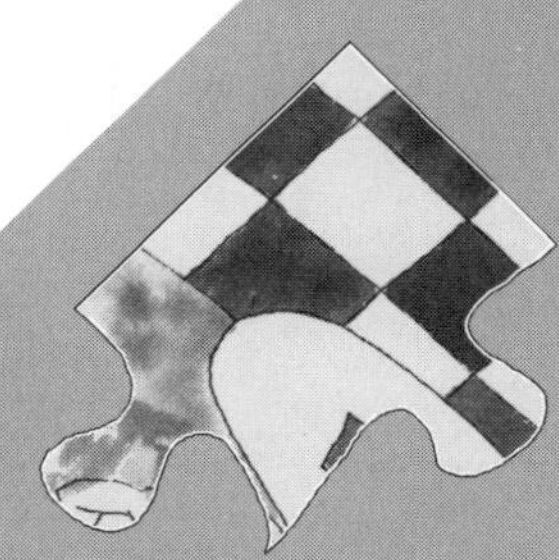

Puzzle

Here's where you glue or paste the puzzle pieces you cut out. When you put them all in place, you'll see your secret message.

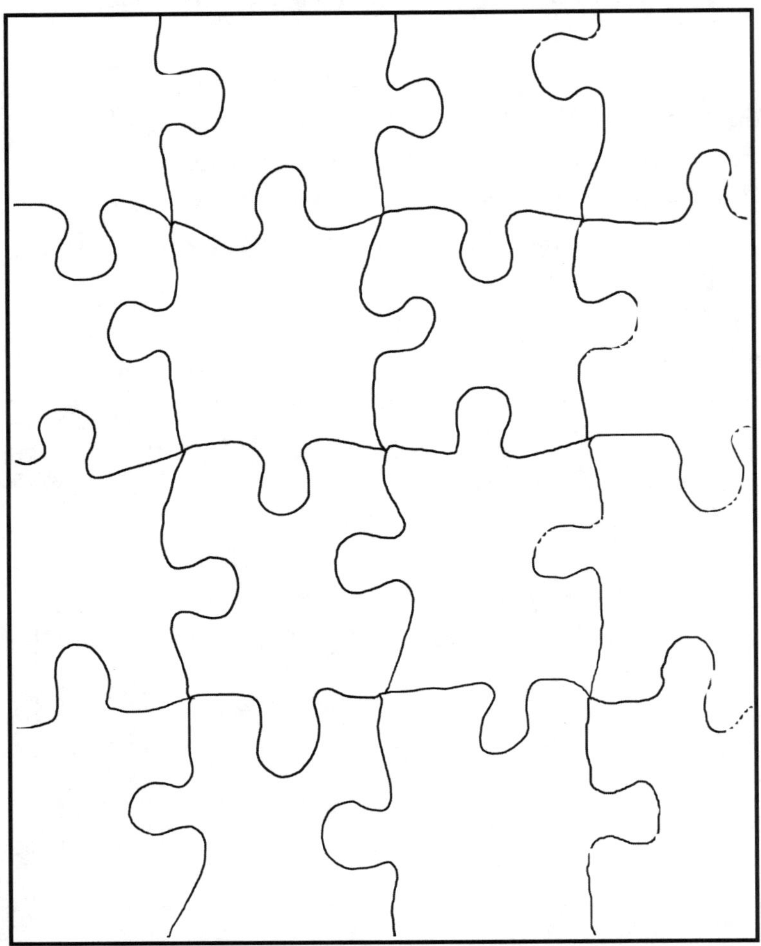

Answers

Page 1

1. Crazy snakes chase brave maids.
2. Sad crabs tap bad rap.
3. Six fish kiss big lips.
4. Shy flies hide five times.
5. Green beans meet sweet peas.

Page 2

START

snow	bricks	candy	sunshine	jewel
right	twins	trail	nap	case
puppy	lips	class	slide	crash
tent	table	beast	dip	plant
print	bread	trick	straw	clown
star	list	nose	button	mouse
glass	flag	prize	laugh	pet

MILK

FINISH

Page 3

campsite, tents, marshmallows, mountains, picnic, river, bear, helicopter, pilot, binoculars

Page 4

our-hour, whole-hole, one-won, buy-by, night-knight, blue-blew

Page 5

The following pairs are synonyms: big-large, yell-shout, loud-noisy, nice-kind, little-small, beautiful-pretty. These pairs are antonyms: happy-sad, slow-fast, over-under, wet-dry.

Page 6

B	A	C	K	P	A	C	K	L	S	F
O	A	C	F	S	G	H	L	M	U	I
O	B	B	A	T	H	T	U	B	N	N
K	U	D	U	T	R	I	N	N	G	G
M	A	I	L	M	A	N	C	O	L	E
A	W	E	C	A	Z	J	H	P	A	R
R	A	I	N	B	O	W	B	Q	S	P
K	X	E	D	B	Y	K	O	F	S	R
P	A	N	C	A	K	E	X	G	E	I
L	A	M	P	S	H	A	D	E	S	N
B	R	D	S	P	Q	E	A	D	A	T
L	T	S	A	F	K	A	E	R	B	H

Page 7

Sample answers:

2. The bubble will burst all over Ming Li's face.
3. Brooke will fall in the ditch.
4. The cake will taste awful.
5. Todd will tip over and spill milk all over himself.
6. Mary Alice will slip on the peel and land in the puddle.

Page 8

Sample summary:

The gorilla took the zookeeper's keys and let all the animals out of their cages. They followed us back to the bus, but our teacher put the animals back in their cages.

Page 9

Day 1: The effect: We didn't get to the World o' Wax Balls today.

Day 2: The cause: I ate 25 chocolate chip pancakes. The effect: Now, I don't feel so good.

Day 3: The cause: . . .my dad slipped and did a belly flob in the tub. The effect: We didn't get to see wax balls being made.

Day 4: The cause: Her finger got stuck in the ball. The effect: When she got up, she had a wax bowling pin stuck on her head.

Page 10

Sample title: Choosing a President

NEWS

School elections are on Wednesday, and there are three students running for president. Before you decide who to vote for, read about each candidate.

Sam Noodle wants to bring new pastas to our school, including spinach fettucine and pepper linguini. He hopes to serve macaroni and cheese at snack time. Sam also wants to add a weekly cooking class. He hopes to improve the quality of food in our school.

Patricia Cooke, (otherwise known as PC) has a real thing for computers. She plans to ask the principal for a new computer for each classroom. PC wants to set up a computer lab for students who want extra computer time. She also hopes to publish a weekly newsletter with computer tips.

Jennie Longshot has already begun a fundraising effort for new sports equipment for the gym. She spoke with the owner of a local sneaker store who says he will give free sneakers to any student who participates in Jennie's jogging class. Jennie wants to help students stay fit. She has even organized daily after-school fitness activities.

Page 11

1: The batter got hit by the ball.
2: The batter will not celebrate. He lost the game.

Page 12

Superball Bill: opinion
A Proud Owner: fact
Chew Gumball: fact
S.O. Nice: opinion

Page 13

Alissa will be nine.

Pages 14–15

Step 1: Answers will vary.
Step 3: We arrived at our campsite on a Saturday afternoon. As soon as we got there, we set up our tents. The first day we went swimming in the lake. Swimming made us tired, so we cooked dinner and then got ready to go to sleep. We heard a noise and watched quietly as a bear came out of the woods. Finally, when the bear left, we were able to go to sleep. The second day we hiked up a mountain. At the top of the mountain, we built a fire and cooked hot dogs. Our legs were so tired that night that we just laid under the stars and told scary stories. It was a terrific campout!

Pages 16–17

1. Plot—At a sleepover, Harry and Jonah play practical jokes on Harry's sister Eloise, but before the night is over she ends up scaring them.
2. Characters—Harry, Jonah, Eloise
3. Setting—Harry's house late at night

Page 18

1. Ronnie the Robot
2. Factoid Fred
3. Ronnie the Robot
4. Factoid Fred
5. Factoid Fred
6. Factoid Fred

Page 19

Answers will vary.

Page 20

The Garden:

The flowers were blooming
Green and red
Filling the earth with color.
Each morning the little girl watered the plants.
So they would bloom all spring.

The Sneeze:

"Achoo," said the boy.
His nose it did drip.
He reached for a tissue
And wiped off his lip.

Page 21

Circle all paragraphs in left column. X all paragraphs in right column.

Page 22

The real librarian: Mr. Best.

Page 23

Answers will vary.

Page 24

Nick: Who hit the final shot in tonight's game ___?___
Coach: Jumpshot Jesse hit a perfect 3-pointer ___.___
Nick: And who scored the most points ___?___
Coach: Freddy Finefinger was our high scorer this time ___.___
Nick: How did the rest of the team play ___?___
Coach: It was a pretty weak night for the first team ___.___ Ryan the Rim Man was taken out of the game because of a twisted ankle ___.___ We really missed him ___.___ If it hadn't been for Jumpshot and Finefinger, we would definitely have lost the game ___.___ What a tragedy that would have been ___.___ We were able to pull it out in the last 3 minutes, though ___. or !___
Nick: Wow ___!___ What an exciting night ___!___
Coach: You said it ___!___ And now we're on our way to the finals ___. or !___ Will you be attending our game in Denver ___?___
Nick: I'll be there to cover the BIG WIN ___!___

Page 25

Mom and I are planning a great surprise for Sal's birthday. We're going to take her to Bongo's Jungle for the whole day. First I'm going to pretend to have a fight with her. When she gets good and mad, Mom's going to tell her that we have to spend the day at Crazy Aunt Ida's. In the car I'll play the music really loud. She'll get so frustrated that she'll put a blanket over her head. When we arrive at Bongo's, she'll look out from under the blanket and scream. She loves the waterslide and Hippo's Harbor ride. She also loves the foot-long hot dogs and wild berry ice-cream sodas. Mom promised to pay for all the tickets, but I'm going to buy lunch. I sure hope Sal is surprised.

Page 26

1. Deserts, are
2. People, build
3. Great Basin, is
4. winds, form
5. cactus, is
6. Lizards, hide

Southwest

Page 27

my aunt: Aunt Rose
a city: New York
a building: The Empire State Building
a museum: The Natural History Museum
a park: Central Park
a man: Arnie Warznegger
a woman: Michelle Fife
a movie: *Killer Kong*
my school: Jefferson School
my best friend: Jamal

Page 28

Answers will vary.

Page 29

1. snack
2. is resting
3. smile
4. sleeps
5. run
6. roars
7. are
8. eats
9. pounds

Page 30

Answers will vary.

Page 31

Dear TV Agent,

I have been acting since I was a young child. My first role was in the second grade play. I played three different parts. I was a snowflake, a princess, and a tree. How's that for real acting? My mom thought I was terrific. Do you want to call and ask her about my performance?

Years later I sang in the Thanksgiving pageant at the mall. Wow, was it exciting! I had the most important part in the pageant. I played a turkey running away from a farmer. Have you ever heard anyone sing and cluck at the same time?

I haven't done much acting since then, but I would sure like a chance to work with you. You see, I'm a natural. Are you ready to put me to work?

Your friend,
Daisy

Page 32

Words capitalized: The United States, You, Hawaii, Pacific Ocean, Or, Mississippi River, Spend, Lake Itasca, If, Erie Canal, Perhaps, Loon Mountain, New Hampshire, Let, Just, Trent Travel, If, Travis

Page 33

2. he's
3. you're
4. X
5. she's
6. X
7. I'll
8. X
9. they'd
10. they're
11. X
12. can't
13. X
14. she'll
15. aren't
16. won't
17. it's
18. shouldn't
19. we're
20. I'm

Page 34

Sample answers:
When Ben was at bat, he was surprised to see a bat overhead.
We had to park three blocks away from the park.
Sara used her hands to block the block.

Page 35
Sample answers:
prefixes: undo, unhappy, unpack, unwind, unsafe, repack, review, recook, rewind, preview, precook
suffixes: happily, safely, doable, viewable, cookable, packable, viewing, cooking, winding
prefixes and suffixes: unhappily, rewinding, unsafely, unwinding, previewing, precooking

Page 36
a. 3
b. 4
c. 2
d. 1

Page 37

1.	oven	**6.**	spoon
2.	hands	**7.**	chips
3.	measuring cup	**8.**	pan, cookies
4.	bowl	**9.**	minutes
5.	cut	**10.**	cookies

Picture should show chocolate chip cookies.

Page 38
2. swims like a fish.
3. hard as a rock.
4. eats like a horse.
5. quiet as a mouse.
6. white as snow.

Page 39
Answers will vary, but sample answers include:

1.	cheesecake	**6.**	wander wistfully
2.	potato pancakes	**7.**	buzzed
3.	thanked them	**8.**	hissed
4.	sings songs	**9.**	growled
5.	frogs found food	**10.**	popped

Page 40
1. C
2. O
3. M
4. P
5. A
6. R
7. I
8. S
9. O
10. N
11. S

Page 41
P P
I I
E E

Page 42

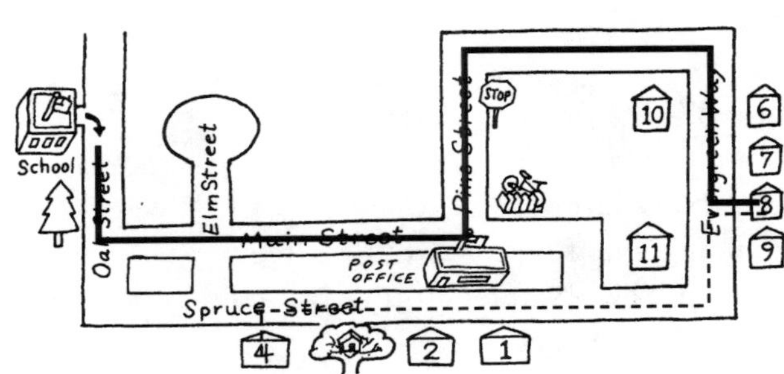

1. 8
2. 4

Page 43
Answers will vary.

Pages 44–45
1. c
2. a
3. f
4. g
5. e
6. h
7. b
8. d

Pages 46–47
Who—Nina and Mark Glass
What—found a treasure
When—yesterday afternoon
Where—Sands Point Beach

Why—they were building a sand castle
How—digging in the sand, noticed something shiny

Pages 48–49
Answers will vary.

Page 50
Answers will vary.

Page 51
The following sentences should be checked:
1, 2, 5, 6, 8.

Page 52

1. I didn't mean to miss practice, but it just couldn't be helped.
2. After school today, I was really hungry, so I went to get a snack.
3. When I finished my snack, I realized I didn't have my sneakers, and I didn't know where they were.
4. I looked everywhere, but I couldn't find them.
5. I went straight to the phone, and I called my mom.
6. She said she could bring me another pair of sneakers, or she could help me find my old ones.

Page 53
Answers may vary, but one possible rewrite is:

Summer camp was so much fun. Sunday night was the annual Water Balloon War. I was the captain of the Tornadoes this year. The other team was the Hurricanes.

Monday morning was the big swim competition. We had the best swimmer, Frank E. Fish, on our team. Monday afternoon we practiced our songs for that night's singing competition. After the show, it was time for the jello-eating contest. I won this, too.

Tuesday was the day for soccer games, volleyball games, and relay races. That night the judges announced the winning team.

Thanks for letting me come to camp again, Mom. It turned out to be the best year ever!

Page 54
Sample answers:

1. I nearly missed Uncle Dave's phone call when he invited me to go fishing.
2. I quickly gathered my rod, hook, and bait.
3. I ran happily down to the pond.
4. Uncle Dave was already waiting with his equipment
5. We successfully baited out hooks and dropped our lines into the water.
6. My line started to slowly quiver.
7. Then it shook strongly.
8. Finally Uncle Dave helped me steady it.
9. I had caught a huge fish which we gladly ate for dinner.

Page 55
Items should be labeled:
John's book
Marcia's cap
the 5th grade boys' football
my teacher's purse
Ms. Jackson's glasses
the coaches' whistles
our principal's briefcase

Page 56
Answers will vary.

Page 57
Armadillos, Vol. A–B
Bridges, Vol. A–B
Cameras, Vol. C–CH
Computers, Vol. Ci–Cz
Crocodiles, Vol. Ci–Cz
Earthquakes, Vol. E–F
Environment, Vol. E–F
Machines, Vol. M–N

Ocean Life, Vol. O-P
Planets, Vol. O-P
Plants, Vol. O-P
Rivers, Vol. Q-R
Soils, Vol. S-T
Tornadoes, Vol. S-T
Volcanoes, Vol. U-V
Water, Vol. W-X

Page 58

1. D	**5.** A
2. T	**6.** D
3. E	**7.** T
4. A	**8.** E

Page 59

1. Custards and Creams, Frostings
2. 27, 30
3. b

Page 60

1. shooting star/Shoshone
2. A briefly visible meteor
3. shə-shṓn- ē
4. Answers will vary.

Page 61

1. D volume
2. no, this encyclopedia is the 1996 edition
3. 21 years old
4. Bullfighting, MVP Bullfighters, Bullfighting Tournaments

Page 62

1. 100
2. Tuesday, Thursday and Saturday
3. end
4. Saturday, 5 more

Page 63

Answers will vary.

How Do You Foster Your Child's Interest in Learning?

In preparing this series, we surveyed scores of parents on this key question. Here are some of the best suggestions:

- Take weekly trips to the library to take out books, and attend special library events.
- Have lots of books around the house, especially on topics of specific interest to children.
- Read out loud nightly.
- Take turns reading to each other.
- Subscribe to age-appropriate magazines.
- Point out articles of interest in the newspaper or a magazine.
- Tell each other stories.
- Encourage children to write journal entries and short stories.
- Ask them to write letters and make cards for special occasions.
- Discuss all the things you do together.
- Limit TV time.
- Watch selected programs on TV together, like learning/educational channels.
- Provide project workbooks purchased at teacher supply stores.
- Supply lots of arts and crafts materials and encourage children to be creative.
- Encourage children to express themselves in a variety of ways.
- Take science and nature walks.
- Teach children to play challenging games such as chess.
- Provide educational board games.
- Supply lots of educational and recreational computer games.
- Discuss what children are learning and doing on a daily basis.
- Invite classmates and other friends over to your house for team homework assignments.
- Keep the learning experiences fun for children.
- Help children with their homework and class assignments.
- Take trips to museums and museum classes.
- Visits cities of historical interest.
- Takes trips to the ocean and other fun outdoor locations (fishing at lakes, mountain hikes).

- Visit the aquarium and zoo.
- Cook, bake, and measure ingredients.
- Encourage children to participate in sports.
- Listen to music, attend concerts, and encourage children to take music lessons.
- Be positive about books, trips, and other daily experiences.
- Take family walks.
- Let children be part of the family decision-making process.
- Sit down together to eat and talk.
- Give a lot of praise and positive reinforcement for your child's efforts.
- Review child's homework that has been returned by the teacher.
- Encourage children to use resources such as the dictionary, encyclopedia, thesaurus, and atlas.
- Plant a vegetable garden outdoors or in pots in your kitchen.
- Make each child in your family feel he or she is special.
- Don't allow children to give up, especially when it comes to learning and dealing with challenges.
- Instill a love of language; it will expose your child to a richer thought bank.
- Tell your children stories that share, not necessarily teach a lesson.
- Communicate your personal processes with your children.
- Don't talk about what your child did not do. Put more interest on what your child did do. Accept where your child is at, and praise his or her efforts.
- Express an interest in children's activities and schoolwork.
- Limit TV viewing time at home and foster good viewing habits.
- Work on enlarging children's vocabulary.
- Emphasize learning accomplishments, no matter how small.
- Go at their own pace; People learn at different rates.
- Challenge children to take risks.
- Encourage them to do their best, not be the best.